UFO
in

MW00957323

Richard Dolan Press
Rochester, New York 14619
USA

Library of Congress Cataloging-in-Publication Data

Dolan, Richard Michael
        UFOs and Disclosure in the Trump Era / by Richard M.
    Dolan
    86 p.   cm.
    ISBN 978-1544748719
    1. Unidentified Flying Objects
    2. History.
    I. Dolan, Richard M. II. Title

First published in the United States by Richard Dolan Press

Manufactured in the United States of America

First Printing: March 2017

UFOs and Disclosure in the Trump Era

Richard Dolan Lecture Series

By Richard Dolan

Richard Dolan Press

2017

Also by Richard Dolan:

UFOs and the National Security State: Chronology of a Cover-Up, 1941-1973

UFOs and the National Security State: The Cover-Up Exposed, 1973-1991

A.D. After Disclosure: When the Government Finally Reveals the Truth about Alien Contact (with Bryce Zabel)

UFOs for the 21ˢᵗ Century Mind: A Fresh Guide to an Ancient Mystery

The Secret Space Program and Breakaway Civilization

Contents

Introduction

The subject of UFOs is endlessly varied and complex. Any one of its subsets can occupy a mind for a lifetime. The scientific and technological complexities, the military encounters, investigations of sightings and encounters, the abduction phenomenon, social and psychological facets, questions about "ancient aliens" and much more.

One of these elements, and the one that has occupied me more than any other, is the political dimension of the UFO phenomenon, specifically the cover-up. For many years, I have argued that military and intelligence agencies have concealed information on UFOs.[1] If you believe the phenomenon is real, it is not difficult to conclude that there is a cover-up concerning it. It follows, too, that you might believe something of very great importance is being withheld from the world, and you might wonder how things would be different if that secrecy ever were lifted. In the field of ufology, that's disclosure.

I have been part of the discussion on disclosure more or less since the phrase became common usage at the beginning of the century. To answer what disclosure means sometimes depends on who you talk to. But generally, most of us have worked on an assumption that it involves a truthful explanation of the situation from those in possession of the secret. A complete end of the secrecy. Cards fully on the table.

It's a reasonable way to look at the matter, but over time I have developed an alternative view. By the time I co-authored *A.D. After Disclosure* in 2010, I fully believed that the political

---

[1] For more information, see http://richarddolanpress.com

authorities were unlikely to go about the process honestly.[2] That if disclosure were to come any time soon, it would be as the result of some unexpected development or accident forcing the hand of the secret keepers. That being so, the process would be dominated by spin, deception, and probably outright lies. It would be the people's job to fight for the truth about UFOs, and they would need to pry the lid open with all of their intelligence and outrage against a black budget establishment that would try to maintain as much control over the information as possible. In the end, I felt, truth would be the most likely outcome—although it could take a while.

Since then, my thoughts have continued to evolve. This booklet is developed from a series of lectures I have given between 2015 and 2017, and the germ of it goes back still several years earlier. From the "accidental" disclosure initially envisioned in *A.D.*, I've come to see four distinct disclosure scenarios. They are based on what I feel is a better and more nuanced understanding of global geopolitics and the global power structure. Our world is constantly changing, and it would be foolish of me to think that, once formulated, my ideas on this most revolutionary of subjects would never need to change.

During 2016, the world experienced several unexpected political events that presented a potential obstacle to the machinery of neoliberal globalization. One was the Brexit vote, in which the British people voted to leave the European Union. The other was the election of Donald Trump to the Presidency of the United States. As of this writing, it is far too early to tell whether these will mean anything in the long term. Both,

---

[2] See Dolan, Richard M. and Zabel, Bryce, *A.D. After Disclosure: When the Government Finally Reveals the Truth About Alien Contact* (New Page Books, 2012).

however, were unpleasant surprises for the global political and financial establishment. This is not to place a value judgment on either of those developments. After all, our world is not black-and-white. But Brexit and Trump may each present opportunities that did not seem previously obvious.

I have sought to incorporate this new reality into the broader discussion of disclosure. Hopefully, it will add to a deepened understanding to some of the most fascinating questions of our time: how does the UFO secret work globally, and what might happen if it were ever to end?

Because this booklet was originally developed from my various lectures on the subject, I have retained the language of my lectures much as possible. Even so, there have been significant edits throughout to improve readability, and I have also added new material to reflect the political realities of America and the world in 2017.

This work is the second in a series of edited transcriptions from selected lectures I have given. An earlier one, titled *The Secret Space Program and Breakaway Civilization*, was published in 2016.

Richard Dolan
Rochester, New York
March 2017

UFOs: What's the Big Deal?

UFO disclosure is not a simple concept. It is layered with meaning deriving from many different disciplines and perspectives. It involves a subject—UFOs—over which no one can agree, and which even experienced students lack a great deal of information in certain areas. Moreover, the results of disclosure are uncertain. Even its desirability is disputed. Yet, I believe in its inevitability.

Before jumping into the nuances and challenges of disclosure, it is worth mentioning that there is a significant mass of confirmed, declassified documentation proving that the subject of UFOs has been and continues to be taken seriously at high levels within the national security apparatuses of many nations. Most prominently by the United States, still the world's most powerful nation and the one that continues to matter most in any discussion about disclosure.

To curious skeptics wondering what's the big deal with UFOs, I would encourage them to read some of the declassified literature on the subject. For many years on my own website, I have had an article entitled "Twelve Government Documents that take UFOs Seriously."[3] These are historical documents released via the United States Freedom of Information Act over the years, primarily during the presidency of Jimmy Carter during the late 1970s. During the early 1980s, President Reagan issued an executive order undercutting (although not repealing) FOIA, essentially making it more expensive and less responsive to the public. These documents, however, remain available. Of the thousands of pages available now there is not a single released document that absolutely proves UFOs are extraterrestrial. But there are a top dozen, a top 50, a top 100 UFO documents that do prove—they do not hint, they do not suggest,

---

[3] "Twelve Government Documents that Take UFOs Seriously," at http://richarddolanpress.com.

but they prove—that the UFO subject has been taken seriously and has represented a genuine concern to military agencies around the world, particularly to the United States. In my "Twelve Documents" article, I assess each of them and explain why they matter.

Gleaning a few highlights from the mass of documentation that exists will only give a sense of the situation, but that will suffice. All of these are well known to UFO researchers; few if any are well known outside that restricted field.

The memo from three-star general Nathan Twining, head of Air Material Command (AMC) at Wright Field (later Wright-Patterson Air Force Base), expressed the problem of "flying saucers" very clearly and starkly. Responding to the query of another general, Twining wrote on September 23, 1947 that "the phenomenon is real not visionary or fictitious." That alone is important, considering that all summer long the Air Force had been telling the world exactly the opposite. But he went on to describe specific characteristics of the craft that had been observed by military personnel and civilians alike. He wrote about:

- "extreme rates of climb, maneuverability ... and action which must be considered evasive when sighted."
- "metallic or light reflecting surface."
- "absence of trail."
- "circular or elliptical in shape, flat on bottom and domed on top."
- "well-kept formation of flights."
- normally no sound.

There is a remarkable memo from the FBI dated January 31, 1949 that discusses the recent sightings over such sensitive installation as Los Alamos National Labs and the Oak Ridge Nuclear Facility. It states:

> this matter [flying saucers] is considered top secret by Intelligence Officers of both the Army and the Air Forces.... During the past two months various sightings of unexplained phenomena have been reported.

A remarkable report concerning unexplained overflights of the Hanford Atomic Energy Commission facility in the state of Washington reads:

> Since 30 July 1950 objects, round in form, have been sighted over the Hanford AEC plant.... Air Force jets attempted intercept with negative results. All units including the anti-aircraft battalion, radar units, Air Force fighter squadrons, and the Federal Bureau of Investigation have been alerted for further observation. The Atomic Energy Commission states that the investigation is continuing....

One of the most important of these early documents came from the CIA. On December 4, 1952, the Director of Scientific Intelligence for the CIA, H. Marshall Chadwell, wrote to his boss, CIA Director Walter Bedell Smith. The year had been filled with dramatic sightings, many of which received public attention, others simply being taken seriously within the classified world:

> At this time, the reports of incidents convince us that something is going on which must have immediate attention.... Sightings of unexplained objects at great altitudes and traveling at high speeds in the vicinity of major U.S. defense installations are of such nature that they are not attributable to natural phenomena or known types of aerial vehicles.

These early documents give a smattering of the attitudes being taken by at least some of the classified world, and as we can see, at times extremely prominent members within that world. It is worth emphasizing again that these documents came to us through an accident of history: the Freedom of Information Act. Even so, FOIA is not a panacea. A great deal remains off-limits to researchers, and documents of higher levels of classifications (top secret or beyond) are almost never released.

In more recent years, the statements from prominent military, intelligence, and government bodies have continued. The French COMETA Report from 1999 is a case in point. This was a 90-page study of UFOs undertaken over several years by an

3

independent group of former officials at the French Institute of Advanced Studies for National Defense, and by experts from various fields. Before its was released, it was sent to French President Jacques Chirac and Prime Minister Lionel Jospin. The report was entitled *UFOs and Defense: What must we be prepared for? ("Les Ovni Et La Defense: A quoi doit-on se préparer?").*[4]

> They demonstrate the almost certain physical reality of completely unknown flying objects with remarkable flight performances and noiselessness, apparently operated by intelligent [beings].

The conclusion of the report is of significance, as well.

> We are currently not aware of the extent of knowledge that U.S. military personnel have gleaned from all of the studies that they have conducted on this subject either based on sightings or, as has sometimes been written, based on materials that they have allegedly recovered.
>
> Whatever the case, it is clear that the Pentagon has had, and probably still has, the greatest interest in concealing, as best it can, all of this research, which may, over time, cause the United States to hold a position of great supremacy over terrestrial adversaries, while giving it a considerable response capacity against a possible threat coming from space.
>
> Within this context, it is impossible for them to divulge the sources of this research and the goals pursued, because that could immediately point any possible rivals down the most beneficial avenues. Cover-ups and disinformation (both active as well as passive) still remain, under this hypothesis, an absolute necessity.
>
> Thus, it would appear natural that in the minds of U.S. military leaders, secrecy must be maintained as long as possible.
>
> Only increasing pressure from public opinion, possibly supported by the results of independent researchers, by more or less calculated disclosures, or by a sudden rise in UFO manifestations, might perhaps induce U.S. leaders and persons of authority to change their stance.
>
> It does not seem that we have arrived at that point yet.

The mass of declassified literature and studies like the COMETA Report surely indicate a high level of seriousness of UFOs, as well as the inexplicable nature of the phenomenon.

---

[4] See The COMETA Report part one and part two at
http://ufoévidence.org.

Inexplicable in terms of conventional technology. However, not so inexplicable if we consider that the source of this is from another civilization.

Of course, I have gone over the historical significance of the UFO phenomenon in much greater detail in my full-length books, most notably volumes one and two of *UFOs and the National Security State*. The subject is important. It is up to us as engaged citizens to find out why.

Having gotten that out of the way, let us attempt to go behind the secrecy, and to understand as well as possible the most likely scenario relating to the UFO phenomenon, first from the human side and then from the non-human side.

Initiating the Secrecy

One of the key reasons for UFO secrecy is simple. There appear to have been retrievals of these objects. This of course is not admitted by any official government, but the testimony for (multiple) crash retrievals is quite extensive. I believe the Roswell event was the retrieval of a non-human technology. That is my opinion, and I believe the evidence, while not one hundred percent definitive, is very good. There a number of other probable crash retrievals, many of which have been described on the web and particularly in Ryan Wood's very good book on the subject.[5]

Second—and this is provable—there have been military encounters with UFOs. In other words, classified engagements by military aircraft. This includes not only the U.S. but also the Soviet Union/Russia, Britain, Europe, Australia, China. South America, Southern Africa—everywhere. Cases in which jets

---

[5] *Majic Eyes Only: Earth's Encounters with Extraterrestrial Technology*, Wood Enterprises, 2005

have been scrambled to intercept UFOs. Something is going on.

Let us pause here. Let us assume Roswell "happened" and these objects were also being seen over sensitive military and nuclear installations (which they were) and let us say your name happens to be Harry Truman, and you are President of the United States. Your leading generals and advisors tell you, "Sir, not only have we acquired exotic technology that doesn't appear to have come from this civilization, but they seem to be here with some sort of an agenda, and we don't have any control over them."

That is a dramatic reality for you to deal with as President of the most powerful nation on the planet. What would you do? Perhaps if it's you, and not Harry Truman making the decisions, you might think you would tell the world, and perhaps that would be a good thing to do. But Harry Truman would be surrounded by people advising him against this. First of all, they would tell him that if he told the world that this phenomenon was real, and especially if he were to tell the world that America had captured their technology, it would be very difficult not to share that technology with everyone else. The easiest way to keep the technology secret would be to deny the entire phenomenon.

But there was more than technology at issue. If you inform the world that there are non-human beings who have arrived here from elsewhere, do you tell everyone that you have this matter under control? When in fact you do not? Would you tell the world that these beings are not hostile when in fact you would have no idea about their intentions?

It is a difficult situation, and it is not hard to understand why Truman and his people made the decision they made, which was to maintain deep secrecy until further notice. Because in fact the President could not tell the world that we had acquired this

Secretary of Defense James Forrestal and President
Harry Truman. Two men in on the secret.

incredible technology. He could not tell the world that these
objects were loitering in our airspace and observing our most
sensitive installations with total impunity. And he could not tell
the world that he know they were not hostile, especially because
he could not fully predict the public reaction and specifically
the level of panic that would likely occur.

Implementing the Secrecy Plan

In such a situation, it might well seem that the wisest course
would be to gather your top people around you and tell them to
come up with a plan. *Let us figure this out*, you would say. *Who
or what are we dealing with? What do we do with the technology? Can we create anything useful out of it? How bad will the
public panic be? How can we control the media? How do we
manage the universities and other influential institutions?*

Those who think it's impossible to manage the media or
academia should consider the infamous Operation Mockingbird,

a program that was exposed in the 1970s by the Congressional investigation known as the Church Committee, and then by Watergate journalist Carl Bernstein. Mockingbird involved no less than 400 mainstream American journalists secretly working on the CIA payroll, although many researchers believe the number is higher. Although Mockingbird ended years ago, the situation today is worse.

For years after Mockingbird was exposed, the CIA very legalistically stated that it no longer engaged in such paid relationships with journalists. This is a lie, as eloquently expressed by the late Dr. Udo Ulfkotte of Germany, who described how the CIA controlled the European media.[6] Generally speaking, the agency has no need to pay off journalists, who are often happy to climb over each other to develop a relationship with the CIA. And it is not merely the CIA that manipulates the mainstream media. The Pentagon spends billions of dollars every year managing its social profile.[7] This includes more than the Pentagon's longstanding policy of infiltrating mainstream news with retired generals as "consultants." It also includes creating socks, or sock puppets. That is, personalities who inhabit the comments sections of countless news websites. We don't know how many of these trolls are paid Pentagon employees, but some of them are. The point is to influence public opinion in ways favorable to U.S. government policy. Some Americans might consider it galling that their tax dollars fund such deception against them.

All of this simply to demonstrate that control over media has

---

[6] European media writing pro-US stories under CIA pressure - German journo, RT, Oct 18, 2014, YouTube.

[7] Pentagon Spending Billions on PR to Sway World Opinion Fox News, February 05, 2009

not only been possible, but a reality for generations. Despite being the subject of countless books and analyses, it continues to this day while so much of the American public remains oblivious. I should emphasize, that this control does not specifically or necessarily come via the office of the President. Rather, the CIA, Pentagon, and other government bureaucracies call the shots, especially those with ties to Wall Street. These groups constitute what political analysts increasingly refer to as the deep state. I have often referred to a similar nexus of power as the national security state. That is, the true power players that quietly work behind and beyond the official governing structure.

The betrayal of the western media establishment in service to the deep state could be a series of lectures by itself. But let us continue.

Everything that was said about the media can be said about academia. That is, if you need to contain a powerful secret, you need to manage the academic community as well. It is worth remembering that managing media and academia have more benefit than simply containing the UFO issue. Clearly, there are many reasons that it is useful for the deep state to manage these institutions. But the UFO topic is indeed one of those reasons.

When I thought I was on my way to a life in academia back in the 1980s and 1990s, my academic advisor—I am quite convinced—was working in some capacity for the intelligence community, probably the CIA. His father, a fine scholar of the ancient world, had also been an OSS officer during World War II. My advisor himself had served in Vietnam as an intelligence officer and later moved on to the Princeton Institute of Advanced Studies and the London School of Economics, both places under the strong influence of U.S. intelligence.

Such relationships are common in the academic world. There is a revolving door between academia and the national security apparatus. It is not that the CIA controls every professor in the country, obviously not. But it can certainly place enough of its people in strategically important places throughout the academic world to keep matters under control. If an assistant professor at a small college becomes interested in UFOs or some other *verboten* topic, some powerful academician will knock him down.[8]

In earlier years, the person who served this function was Donald Menzel of Harvard University. Menzel was one of the world's leading astronomers and the most prominent debunker of UFOs. His role at Harvard, and the books he wrote on UFOs—all of them very bad and using bad science—were powerfully influential in derailing genuine investigation and discussion of UFOs around the world.

Donald Menzel

We now know that Menzel was much more than an important astronomer at Harvard. He also secretly worked with the NSA in a high-level capacity. In fact, he happened to be one of the world's best cryptographers, which of course is what the NSA is all about. No one, not even his wife, knew Menzel was so prominent within the NSA. Researcher Stanton Friedman found out years after Menzel's death.

There are many deep connections between the national security state and our major public institutions. Such covert

---

[8] A classic study of the relationship of the CIA with one of the leading Ivy League universities—Yale—is by Robin Winks. See Cloak and Gown: Scholars in the Secret War, 1939-1961.

relationships are instrumental in managing the culture and keeping potential troublemakers in line. It does not work perfectly all the time, but it is usually effective. This is what happened in the 1940s, and it is still happening today.

Similarly, the world of science can be, and has been, controlled. Scientific research requires funding. In the United States, the two dominant sources of scientific funding are from industry and government, and by far the largest portion of government funding comes from the Department of Defense. If a certain area of research happens to be classified, then the funding will be classified. Open, public science is tightly controlled.

Creating the Black World

Continuing further with the scenario of developing a UFO secrecy program, we come to the matter of black budgets and black agencies. On one level, black budgets are easy to understand. They are simply classified spending about which members of Congress know little if anything. There might be a vague line in the budget describing a program title. It gets approved, and that's that. These are known as special access programs (SAPs).

Only rarely does one hear much about the size of the black budget. Some estimates have put it at between $30 billion and $50 billion a year.[9] Keep in mind this is merely the classified portion of U.S. defense spending, which is more than the entire military budgets of all but a small handful of nations. In all likelihood, the actual total is higher, because the real black budget includes more than classified tax dollars. The CIA and intelligence community has a long history of involving itself

---

[9] Wikipedia, for example.

with securities fraud, narcotics trafficking, and other forms of financial corruption.[10]

Regarding drug trafficking, for instance, no one knows how big that industry is, but it is one of the most lucrative in the world. In 2003, the United Nations estimated it generated $321 billion that year, or roughly 1% of the global GDP. With annual global GDP in 2017 well over $100 trillion, the illicit narcotics industry is probably now worth over $1 trillion per year. Just because this money is illegal does not make it undesirable. Everyone wants it, whether they are the CIA, the Russian FSB, the Pakistani ISI, Israel's Mossad, or anyone else. If you want to rig elections, raise secret armies, blow up buildings and blame it on terrorists, or—back to our main topic—secretly research UFO-related technology, you will need a great deal of money, and you would not want all of it coming from official (and therefore traceable) tax dollars. The program must remain secret, and therefore the funding must be secret. Drug trafficking and other illegal activities are an important way to facilitate this. No one has ever confirmed that narco money goes into the UFO secrecy program, but it could very well contribute. No matter what, however, there is a black budget supporting *the program*.

So much secret spending, year after year, for ultra secret special access programs relating to UFOs inevitably leads to runaway privatized secrecy. There haven't been many studies of the black budget, but the few that we know about have indicated that we are not dealing a system dominated by the Pentagon *per se*. Rather, it is led by the private defense contractors such as Boeing, Lockheed Martin, Raytheon, General Electric, General

---

[10] Still recommended is Catherine Austin Fitts, "What's Up With the Black Budget? The $64 Question" (2002).

Dynamics, Bechtel, and so on. This is where the money is, and this is where the real power is.[11]

As a society, we have little to no control over this situation. We do not know how many special access programs there are. We do not know who is running them. A number of years ago, there appeared a story about a classification within the U.S. Navy, known as Alternative Compensatory and Control Measures (ACCM). This was one of the names for their deeply classified programs. It turned out that the Navy itself did not have control over what was going on in these programs. Forget Congress—the Navy itself admitted it had lost control.[12]

There are programs that exist off the grid, so to speak, within the military and intelligence community. The problem has gotten to be so immense, so unmanageable, it often seems doubtful that anyone can ever gain control over it.

Weaponizing the Technology

One thing the classified world appears to be doing with UFO technology is weaponizing it. Supporting this assertion is a document known as the Project Condign report, deriving from

---

[11] Sweetman, Bill. "In Search of the Pentagon's Billion Dollar Hidden Budgets. How the U.S. keeps its R&D Under Wraps." *Jane's Information Group*, 5 Jan 2000. Priest, Dana and Arkin, William. "Top Secret America: A Washington Post Investigation." (Three parts) July 19, 2010. See also Priest & Arkin, *Top Secret America: The Rise of the New American Security State* (Little, Brown and Company, 2011).

[12] Kibbe, Jennifer D. "Covert Action and the Pentagon" *Intelligence and National Security*, Vol. 22, No. 1, Feb 2007 pp. 57-74.

the U.K. in the year 2000.[13] My colleague John Burroughs did a great deal of research into this document. Many of us, including myself, overlooked the details in it because it's quite long and very dry. However, it contains critically important information, which incidentally appears to have been declassified by the U.K. government against the wishes of senior members of the intelligence community.

John was in the U.S. Air Force and had been at Rendlesham/Bentwaters in 1980, during one of the most significant UFO events in history, and has suffered issues with his heart and eyesight to this day. Something clearly happened to him at that time, but unfortunately his medical records have been classified.

Within the Condign Report are clear references to UAP (Unexplained Aerial Phenomena, the military phrase for UFO). What initially got his attention was the report's direct reference to the Rendlesham incident, which postulated that this could have "been an example [in which] several observers were probably exposed to UAP radiation for longer than normal UAP sighting periods."

This is a top secret British MOD confirmation of the high strangeness of the Rendlesham encounter. The report discoursed at length on the reality of UAP/UFO phenomena:

It could not be discounted that an extraordinary (even extra-terrestrial) finding can account for some events...

To attain the exceptional aerial performance, based on the reports studied, a UAP vehicle reportedly (but not always) often exhibits both propulsion and aerodynamic characteristics at or beyond the limit of current human design and engineering capability....

Apparently emit some sort of invisible field, which, when in close

---

[13] The full Project Condign report can be downloaded at the Ministry of Defence website under the title "UAP in the UK Air Defence Region: Executive Summary."

proximity, can, reportedly cause humans and equipments to respond in unusual ways. At worst a close range exposure to a UAP can cause some disturbing mental and physical effects ...

There are also references in the report to the desirability of weaponizing UAP/UFO technology, especially with regards to plasma and magnetic fields. The report recommended "further investigation [be undertaken] into the applicability of various characteristics in various novel military applications."

It is interesting that officially speaking, and as reported by most of the media, the report tries to explain UAP on bizarre and poorly understood weather phenomena such as ball lightning. What not discussed is how these terrifying effects from highly localized weather anomalies would cause pilots to take extreme evasive action, expose witnesses to harmful radiation, and cause such psychological effects as hallucinations and missing time events.

During 2016, I was fortunate to meet one of the authors of the Condign report. He told me there was no question whatsoever that he and his team knew the UAP phenomenon was generated by a non-human intelligence. This was not considered to be a bizarre weather phenomenon, he said, but aliens. Moreover, he said that weaponizing this technology was considered of paramount importance.

Of course this makes perfect sense. These are military people. If they acquire exotic technology, or if they have access to studying it, they will seek to create weapons out of it. It is interesting, also, that the Condign report briefly discussed analyses of UAP by other nations. One statement mentioned that there was "no formal intelligence exchange on this topic." This would seem surprising, but the key word here is "formal." The paper does go on, however, indicating that at least some people in the classified world are keeping their finger on the pulse of this subject to check for global trends. "However [redacted on the basis of international relations] are known to have at least one member of staff active in this area."

The report specifically mentions the Russians and Chinese in this regard:

> Russian, Former Soviet Republics and Chinese authorities have made co-ordinated effort to understand the UAP topic.... Russian investigators have measured 'fields' which are reported to have caused human effects when they are located close to the phenomenon.

It is not surprising that the Russians and Chinese would be interested in studying UAP/UFO every bit as much as their western counterparts. After all, both have had their own long history of UFO encounters. It is important, however, that this classified report appears to confirm the matter. It is fair to assume that there is something of a global competition in researching UFO-related technologies.

A Secret Space Program

Moving on with our understanding of the "big picture," there is the matter of clandestine breakthroughs in research and technology that lead to money and power. Claims have existed—difficult to prove—that high tensile fibers, fiber optics, and more came ultimately from the study of crashed UFOs. My friend Dr. Bob Wood believes, and I believe he made a good case, that the transistor itself, patented in 1947, might derive from the crash of a UFO at Cape Girardeau, Missouri, in 1941. For me, it comes down to this: if there were retrievals of crashed UFOs, and I believe there were, then it would make sense that this has had an effect on our technological development.

Such breakthroughs, both technologically and in the realm of cosmology, lead logically to a breakaway civilization. This is because some clandestine breakthroughs would simply be too important to release to the rest of the world—for example, energy or propulsion breakthroughs. It is not hard to understand why such developments would be kept secret. If the long-suspected breakthrough in the area of electogravitics or field propulsion (e.g. antigravity), really has been achieved, it would be a truly revolutionary development. Rather than fly for sixteen hours from Vancouver to Sydney, wouldn't it be so much more convenient to do it in a fraction of the time in your own flying saucer? If people had the ability to do that, that means a great deal of power, a great deal of freedom.

The implications would be greater still if such new forms of propulsion were derived from a non-petroleum based source. In 2013, I attended a free energy conference in Boulder, Colorado and met some fascinating researchers. I learned there are many brilliant people in this world who are thinking about energy breakthroughs. I cannot know if all of their ideas are valid, but it seems likely to me that some of them are.

If so, we must assume that the classified world, with far greater money and security, has learned most of the important ones and have classified them. If the people had access to an energy breakthrough—for instance, a device that would allow you to go off the energy grid—that's more freedom and more power for the people. Such breakthroughs are dangerous from the perspective of those at the summit of our power structure. It is dangerous because fundamentally we are dealing with the theft of our planet by a few people at the top of our power structure. The release of radical technologies to the people would disrupt the achievement of that goal. Energy and propulsion breakthroughs are two such ways to do this.

Most probably, then, key breakthroughs within the classified world would be hidden, but of course research would continue. Considering the sightings of unusual technology at black budget sights near the infamous Area 51, Antelope Valley, Dugway

Proving Ground, and elsewhere, I think this is what people are observing. It would appear that such breakthroughs have involved the development of what can only be called flying saucers. Could such vehicles leave Earth's atmosphere and go elsewhere? I believe this is so, and this would therefore constitute a secret space program.

Photograph from the edge of Area 51, February 1990.

There is unfortunately a proliferation of the current group of self-described whistleblowers who have talked about going to Mars. None of those individuals have offered stories that can be corroborated, much less documented or proven. Genuine whistleblowers provide information that can be checked in one way or another. On top of this, the Mars stories go beyond describing advanced technology and regularly delve into the magical, such as time travel and even reverse aging. It is not that such claims are *a priori* always impossible. But they are incredibly unlikely and always incredibly convenient for the storyteller, as their stories can never be fact-checked. After all, if your own family never knew you left for Mars because after twenty years on Mars you were reverse time traveled back into your teenage house and teenage body .... at this point, words fail the rational investigator. The most important revelation from these stories is how gullible so many people can be, and of course how willing a few individuals are to take advantage of that.

As an aside, I should add that if I were managing security for a secret space program, I would want to litter the research field with nonsense. I would search for people who say things that are literally incredible, and ensure they get in front of others who would video record them and publicize them. There are certainly people connected to the UFO research field who are willing to interview anyone with a story. The intelligence community, moreover, has had a long history of disinformation relating to UFOs. In summary, please do not believe every single thing that comes across your Facebook feed.

Having said that, there are genuine whistleblowers. Donna Hare, for instance, worked in the 1970s for the NASA subcontractor Philco Ford. She is a real person who has a confirmable work history. She described how NASA regularly airbrushed photographs of the Moon in order to remove images of UFOs. I also credit whistleblowers such as Karl Wolff, who was in the U.S. Air Force at Wright Patterson Air Force Base during the 1960s. Wolff discussed images he saw that depicted structures on the Moon. I also believe that there are quite a few anomalies in Earth orbit that signify an infrastructure that is not supposed to exist, but does. There is something going on.

There may very well be something interesting going on with Mars. I once had a conversation with a brilliant scientist who told me early on in my research not to discount the Mars anomalies. There are those of us, he said to me, who are looking at those anomalies very carefully. This is someone with an outstanding resume in the classified world. Based on his statement, along with so many other leaks, I conclude that it is very likely—a virtual certainty—that a secret space program exists.

Desperately Trying to Catch Up

It is rational to assume that the military-minded people involved in the black budget breakaway civilization are desperately trying to catch up to the *others*—whoever and whatever they are. I have concluded for some time that this group is very possibly splintered and in some kind of competition with each other. This would presumably involve the Russian and Chinese as well as other groups.

A few years ago I received an email from someone who positioned himself as someone with inside classified budget experience and knowledge of the advanced, exotic programs related to extraterrestrials. I don't know who he was, but he was clearly very intelligent. He told me that he had read my book *A.D. After Disclosure*, which he said was interesting but overlooked something important. He believed that I did not appreciate how panicked and frightened his group was by the prospect of the secret getting out. He emphasized that there would be little chance of any cooperation from the black world on this subject unless his group was certain that the people involved in the secrecy would not be prosecuted by an angry public. In fact, I did discuss this in the book, and agree with him fully. There is undoubtedly much fear among those in the know on what would happen once the secret is out.

Ultimately, however, I believe there is a bigger fear within that secret world. These are the revolutionary implications of a true disclosure of the UFO reality—the main theme of *After Disclosure*. Can anyone truly imagine how a U.S. President would tell the world? *It has come to my attention that UFOs are real. Okay, great! I'm going on vacation, see ya later!*

No doubt, any President would want to go on a long vacation after such an announcement, because the follow up questions would be endless and not especially fun. *Does this mean the government has been lying for the last 70 years? How have you been able to perpetrate such a lie? How did you subvert our political institutions, our media, our academic communities, who seem to have been complicit in all this? Tell us more about the black budget world—have you been reverse engineering alien technology? What about the rumors of underground bases?*

Such initial political blowback would just be the beginning. Looming over that would be the potential end of our energy paradigm. After all, once it is acknowledged that this phenomenon is real, it will not be long before people also realize that these objects use something other than petroleum to get from one place to the next. Perhaps something better, whatever that *better* is, and this implies a post-petroleum paradigm to our world. It is the most fundamental transformation of human civilization that I can imagine.

Speculating on the ET Scenario

There is another aspect to this scenario, one that goes beyond human infrastructure. I am speaking of these other beings. Keeping in mind that these are my speculations, I will do my best to ground them in the best reliable evidence and logic.

First, I think they probably came here from elsewhere. Some other place, presumably another world in this universe. I don't know where, and it could be they come from another place in some greater reality that I do not comprehend. What we call another dimension, perhaps. But fundamentally they are not from *here*.

Moreover, they clearly have access to incredibly advanced technology. This has been evident in all the reports we have amassed over the years. From the capability of their craft to accelerate, change shape, disappear, and so on. It is true that our own technology—the official technology that we know about—is becoming more incredible each year. It is possible, even likely, that some of the unknown craft we see today are built within the classified world. But the reports of astonishing technology go very far back. Whoever is operating these objects has knowledge of physical laws that even today we do not seem to have mastered.

One of the amazing things they appear to be able to do is manipulate space-time. We recognize that space-time is not what our common sense tells us. Time is not a river that moves forever in one direction. Nor does space simply expand infinitely in straight lines in all directions. Space and time are intimately connected like a web. They are also affected by gravity. There are enough anomalies both spatially and temporally within the UFO literature that we need to consider the likelihood that these other beings have mastered space-time in some way. But also, if they are coming here from another world, I think it likely that they have learned how to manipulate space-time as a way of traversing the immense interstellar distances. Such a breakthrough in understanding and engineering is not something that, officially at least, we are even remotely able to do.

Another thing about these beings, at least it seems to me, is the likelihood that they are artificially created organisms. They can certainly be biological to a greater or lesser degree. Years ago this would have been considered fantasy. But consider how certain sciences have progressed in the last generation or more: genetics, nanotechnology, computing, artificial intelligence, and so much more.

Ultimately we need to acknowledge that these other beings, whatever their specific agenda may be, have an interest in humanity and the Earth. UFOs have been seen in every part of the world, from the most remote to the most densely populated. There is an infrastructure behind their actions, and a society the likes of which few if any researchers have even the faintest idea.

We can go a little further in speculating about these other beings. There has been serious research into the subject of contact with them, whether through abduction or other forms of communication or observation. Over the years, there have been a very wide number of physical types that have been reported. Realistically, we have no idea how accurate these are. Moreover, if these other beings chose to conceal their true identity and form from us, how difficult would it really be? On the other hand, if they have total genetic mastery, as I have often suggested, then it might be possible that they have created a huge plethora of "types" based on different experiments. We really have no idea.

Having said that, there have been a few basic types that are reported over and over. There are the seemingly ubiquitous Greys. There are beings that are more insect-like, often called Insectoids. There are beings described as reptilian. There are beings that some researchers call the Ebens (who are not quite like Greys but with typically no hair and a large skull). There are also a number of reports of entirely human-looking beings but who are associated with UFO abductions and have been reported on craft, sometimes alongside alien beings. These have sometimes been called the Nordics or Blonds, because they are often reported as having blond hair and nordic appearance.

Whatever amount of truth exists in any of these or other descriptions and types, there does appear to be the intrusion of beings who are not human, and who come from a different civilization. Judging from the entire body of testimony we have, their psychology is truly alien. In their interactions with us, they do not exhibit any of the classically human forms of emotion or interaction. No humor, no conversation, no interest in our hopes or desires, no anger or sadism, no love. Indeed, there is no indication of sex organs in creatures like the Greys.

It is true that there are cases in which abductees will receive an intense feeling of emotion from these beings, sometimes described as love. But this frequently strikes one as intentionally manipulative, just as everything these beings do when they abduct a person. It is also true that some interactions with human-looking operators of UFO craft have been described as fairly ordinary. But of course, those operators were human, and would naturally have our psychology, or at least the basics of our brain chemistry. On the other hand, there have been many encounters with human-looking beings who have most definitely been not like the rest of us. I would only add that if some of these beings are artificially enhanced or designed in some way, they would certainly be very different from us psychologically. Would they have families? Would they have a mother and father who they love, and who loves them? Would they have a sex drive and therefore a desire to find a mate or love? As far as we can tell from the accounts and testimony we have received so far, they seem very different from us in every way imaginable.

They also appear to be powerfully telepathic. Nearly every communication ever reported concerning these beings has *not* involved them opening their mouths and speaking words. They have, on the other hand, nearly all involved telepathic communication of some sort. It seems to me that to the extent they communicate with us, they carefully tailor what they "say" and in all likelihood must be judicious with what they tell us. I spoke with one abductee, a subject in one of the major books on the abductions, who told me his sense is that these beings had a collective mind with no privacy among themselves. Moreover, that they had to slow their minds down considerably in order to communicate with him. This was his impression, at least.

Logically, these beings would have to tailor their message very carefully to us. Presumably, they are a different species, after all. Also, imagine how difficult it would be for human time travelers to go back a mere century and talk about our world to people of that era. How much could we say without causing a complete societal meltdown? If that is difficult to ponder, imagine the problems that a different species with radically different technology would face in talking to us?

There are many more questions we can ask. Most cannot be answered at our current state of knowledge. Did they design us? Do they manage us somehow? Where are they from? What do they want? What kind of society do they have? What is the full extent of their technology and capabilities? We can guess at some of these answers, but that's the best we can do for now.

Layers of Reality

I have come to see the way we perceive reality as a series of concentric circles.

We start out in the center, which I call mass reality. The brightest circle. It is where all the attention is focused. Kim Kardashian's ass, for example, inhabits this region. Football is there, too, along with *Dancingwiththewhatever*. It is the mass culture, dumbdumb reality that bombards us every day. It also includes the idiocy of *CNN* and mainstream news reality, which is the dumbest, most confusing form of so-called news that I can imagine.

One step beyond this is academic reality. The first time you go to university you become aware that there are critiques of culture and society, as well as "alternative" political views, and so on. In fact, most of these critiques and alternative points of

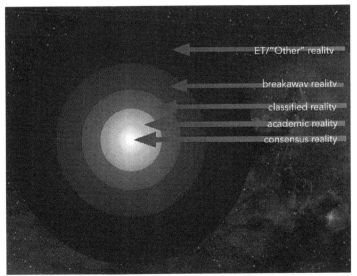

Our five layers of reality.

view are not as insightful as they try to appear. Even so, most people entering the world of academia assume they are seeing beyond the suffocating mass reality. They think, *this is how things really are*. I call this academic reality. It is more sophisticated than mass reality, but still far from the full truth of the reality around us.

Beyond academic reality is something we may call classified reality. The classified world is always beyond the academic world. There are certainly more books written on the CIA today than a few decades ago. Even so, it remains difficult to research deeper levels of reality concerning the CIA for a simple reason: it is the nature of the intelligence world is that if they are doing their job, you are not going to know about it. Scholars know this, of course, but seem to forget this fact in practice. In other words, they know the CIA works in secrecy, but historians and other scholars work with confirmed documents. This of course is essential for the integrity of research, but it becomes a liability when documents are simply not available, and researchers act as though, *if I can't prove it, it doesn't exist.* The prevalent attitude, so it seems to me. It is rather worrisome when we consider the research of Trevor Paglen from his book, *Blank Spots on the Map,* an interesting study of classified U.S. military locations. He estimated that perhaps as much as fifty percent of all U.S. government documents are classified in one form or another. Based on this, one could reasonably argue that half of the activity of the U.S. government is secret.

Beyond the classified reality is what I call the breakaway reality. The classified world is large. But the world that deals with the UFO reality is a very limited part of the classified world. That is way beyond. I've already given my thoughts on that world, so let us move on.

Then beyond the breakaway reality is the reality of these other beings. I imagine it is far beyond even the breakaway civilization.

Driving Our Future

We are moving toward a very wild future. Consider Moore's Law. During the 1960s, Charles Moore of IBM described how every 18 to 24 months the number of transistors in an integrated circuit had doubled. Now interpreted more broadly to describe general computing power, Moore's Law has held true. There is talk that Moore's Law may be reaching its limit, but after fifty years it is still going. Computing power continues to increase explosively.

Hand in hand with this we see revolutionary advances in artificial intelligence, quantum computing, molecular computing, nanotech, robotics, 3-D printing and scanning, DNA mapping, gene editing, and brain mapping.

We are also on the cusp of seeing implants for greater abilities—think super soldiers. Indeed, this is happening now. These will include genetic modifications for intelligence, strength, immunity and so on, presumably if you can afford it. As an aside, the optimism of some of these futurists can be a bit unsettling. Brilliant though Ray Kurzweil is, he conveys pure optimism on matters like human immortality with few if any negative repercussions. Perhaps it is a failure of my own imagination, but I think there may be a number of negative repercussions. In any case, it would seem naive to believe that these breakthroughs will be for everyone. I have a nagging fear that there will be a few people who will be able to leverage this incredible technology for their descendants, but maybe not for yours or mine. It is not hard to see a kind of class-based transhumanism. That is, a frightening version of what Hitler tried to create: a race-based species differentiation in which some people will have genetically designed intelligence, strength, and immunity. In one sense, this is already happening, with an obviously dumbed down culture while the super rich live like gods. But perhaps in the future they will separate themselves further, biologically.

Another technology driving our future is predictive modeling. Think of movies like *Minority Report*, in which future crimes are predicted and "stopped." Alarmingly, something along these lines is happening now. For instance, predictive modeling already occurs based on your web searches and online purchases. Open Google Gmail and you see ads that are custom designed for you, at least to a certain extent, based on your email subject lines. What is interesting is that it is possible for someone with access to this information to create a profile of you. Does anyone have such access? Based on leaks and revelations from whistleblowers like Edward Snowden and more recently via the CIA's Vault7 leaked by Wikileaks, it is evident that government officials and even contractors have access to the records of huge numbers of people. And yet we ourselves do not have access to our own profile. We live in a perverse era in which it is feasible—and even probable in some cases—that a complete stranger knows us better than we know ourselves, all based on our web profile. They know our web history, our email content, our text information, our GPS history, our shopping habits, and so much more. A sophisticated psychological profile can easily be created on every person who has some connectivity to the web, which of course is nearly all of us. This capability will only increase as time goes by.

Then add in such burgeoning technologies as facial and voice recognition, both of which are developing rapidly. Sweeping surveillance and identification systems are coming into place, from street corner cameras to insect drones and beyond, much of which is already connected to a comprehensive database. Let your imagination wander. We are probably a generation away or less from total surveillance of everything that we do.

It won't end with us being watched. Mind reading technologies are being developed. Electrodes can be attached to your skull and algorithms can identify the words you think with 90% percent accuracy. You see, your brain produces certain wavelengths when you think certain words so ... surprise. The current tech is a bit clunky, since it requires that you be thinking actual words, and they still need wires connected to your skull. But it's a start. What is a unnerving is how optimistic some of these articles sound, how happy the authors are that these new technologies can "help" people. How wonderful. Sure, who doesn't want their mind picked open by a futuristic artificially intelligent locksmith?[14]

Beyond even this, we will very soon be seeing ultrafast, ultraintelligent machines, robots, and virtual assistants. Will we even be able to calculate the IQ of these assistants?

This is the future we are moving toward, at least some of the future tech. There are socioeconomic and political developments, too. More on those in a moment.

Disclosure

Let's talk about disclosure now. This subject has become a large part of the discussion on UFOs over the last fifteen years. But even long before that, going back to the 1950s, the subject has been discussed under different names. Back then, the National Investigative Committee on Aerial Phenomena (NICAP), under the leadership of retired Marine Corps Major Donald E. Keyhoe, pressed for an end to UFO secrecy. Among NICAP's board members was former CIA Director Roscoe Hillenkoetter.

The assumption at that time was that the United States had a functioning democratic system. As a result, people could argue that the best tactic for change was by working through Congress, the elected representatives of that system. During the late 1950s and early 1960s, NICAP tried several times to work quietly with certain members of Congress to obtain hearings on

---

[14] Mindsweeper: Reading minds with 90 percent accuracy, by William Saletan. Slate, Mar 28 2008. Reached Via a Mind-Reading Device, Deeply Paralyzed Patients Say They Want to Live, Slashdot Feb 01, 2017. Salih Tutun, Mohammad T. Khasawneh, Jun Zhuang. New framework that uses patterns and relations to understand terrorist behaviors. Expert Systems with Applications, 2017; 78: 358 DOI: 10.1016/j.eswa.2017. 02.029

Admiral Roscoe Hillenkoetter, first Director of the CIA and board member of NICAP. That academic historians ignore his interest in UFOs remains a glaring omission.

the subject of UFOs. Every time, at the 11th hour, the rug was pulled out from beneath them. In retrospect, we can see why this happened: because the U.S. was not a truly democratic system, even then. One of the few people to understand this at the time was C. Wright Mills, one of the great sociologists of the twentieth century. In 1956, he wrote his classic, *The Power Elite*. Americans, argued Mills, liked to think that they possessed a democratic society, but in fact there was a well-defined power structure.

Today of course we now take that as a given. There are countless studies demonstrating that the United States is essentially ruled by an oligarchy—something that applies to most other nations, as well. Laws are passed specifically for those groups with the money and power to wield influence. To the extent that poor people see any laws passed that they actually want, it is only because their interests coincide with those of the powerful.[15]

In fundamentals, we have an authoritarian system, one that is moving toward if not already a form of fascism. Let's call it neofascism, since it is obviously quite different from the 1935 version of fascism that existed in Hitler's Germany. Fascism today cannot look like the 1930s because we are not in the 1930s anymore. No one seeking to create fascism today is so stupid as to call it by that name. They call it "safety" and "protection from hate speech" and "national security" and any number of things. Neofascism today includes entertainment like Monday Night Football and the Academy Awards.

Today, some people are saying that Donald Trump is the new Hitler and that America has now entered fascism. But when a government can read every email you have ever written, GPS you 24/7, place surveillance cameras on every streetcorner, monitor your web traffic, that is fascism. That barn door opened fifteen years ago—it was called the USA PATRIOT Act, and it was passed in Congress after 9/11. Americans have been living in that reality ever since. For those people who now are con-

---

[15] Testing Theories of American Politics: Elites, Interest Groups, and Average Citizens. Martin Gilens and Benjamin I. Page. Published online 18 September 2014. Study: US is an oligarchy, not a democracy, *BBC News*, 17 April 2014. Counter claims surfaced after the Princeton study appeared, arguing that America is more of an "imperfect democracy" than an oligarchy. See Remember that study saying America is an oligarchy? 3 rebuttals say it's wrong. Dylan Matthews, *Vox* May 9, 2016.

cerned about fascism coming to the United States, they might want to examine the structures that have been in place for a very long time. We do not have transparency in government. Instead, we have an opaque government that knows more about us than we know about it.

With such a government as this, how do we achieve disclosure about UFOs? Will it happen by going through Congress? In 2013, I participated in the Citizens Hearing on Disclosure, a week-long event in Washington, D.C. presided over by retired members of Congress. Much of it of course is available on YouTube. I am proud to have been involved in this event because it has left a cultural legacy. But are we really going to achieve disclosure on UFOs by going through Congress? Having spoken to all of those members of Congress, I can say confidently that they did not believe so. They all knew the system was broken.

If we lack a truly representative system, but have something more oligarchic and authoritarian—something neofascist—then how do we achieve a disclosure of the UFO reality? We shall return to this question.

The International Scene

The United States is not the only nation on Earth, and not the only nation that encounters UFOs. Yes, it is still the most powerful nation, and it is critical to understand the role of the U.S. in the overall phenomenon. But there are two hundred other sovereign nations, at least in theory. How does UFO secrecy work internationally?

In the first place, nations aren't what they used to be. The true structure of power today does not rest primarily on nations, but rather a global financial and political elite. They converge at the infamous Bilderberg meetings, in the halls of the Council on

Foreign Relations, at the secretive Bohemian Grove and the like. If you want to see them in action, you can go to the Aspen Institute, which is not much different than an open Bilderberg meeting. You will see the same people discussing the same talking points as in the Bilderberg meetings, but for public consumption, with a large serving of political correctness. Even so, they will tell you their plan for the future. It is a plan in which they are the lords and we and our children and grandchildren are the serfs working for them. It is a global system that will be micromanaged by them because they are convinced that they know how to do this, that they are smart enough, and ultimately have the right to manage you and me.[16]

They certainly need to utilize the power of the United States, which after all has the most dominating military on the planet. This means they must control the U.S. military and intelligence community. It means they must control the black budget agencies within the U.S.—organizations such as the CIA, NSA, NRO, and so on. Many of America's intelligence agencies, including the NSA and NRO, existed in total secrecy for many years. The U.S. has a long tradition of powerful intelligence agencies that do not officially exist, and although I cannot prove a negative, I believe such a tradition continues today.

Working through these intelligence agencies are relationships and partnerships with the equivalent agencies of other nations. For example, there are the so-called Five Eyes. These include U.S., U.K., Canada, Australia, and New Zealand,

---

[16] The definitive book on the Bilderbergers is by Daniel Estulin, *The True Story of the Bilderberg Group*, Trine Day, 2009. A fine review of it is by Stephen Lendman, "The True Story of the Bilderberg Group" and What They May Be Planning Now. A Review of Daniel Estulin's book" at globalresearch.ca.

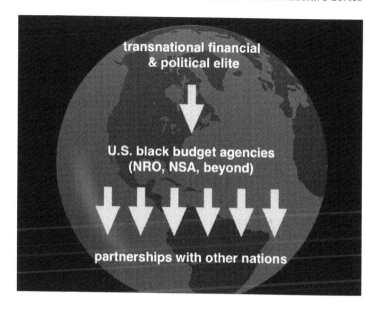

exposed during the 1990s by a New Zealand journalist and at the time described as Project Echelon.[17] Even then, we knew this was a global electronic interception program in which the NSA and its equivalents in other nations shared their data. This enabled them to skirt legal issues about spying on their own population. Britain's GCHQ would spy on the Americans and offer that data to the NSA. Edward Snowden's revelations dovetail with much of this and expand upon it, as do the 2017 revelations of the CIA's Vault7 by Wikileaks. Within this international structure, the U.S. remains first among equals. There is simply so much more money available to the U.S. black budget infrastructure than is available to any other

---

[17] Lucas Matney, Uncovering ECHELON: The Top-Secret NSA/GCHQ Program That Has Been Watching You Your Entire Life, Aug 3, 2015 techcrunch.com.

country. It is what allows the U.S. to be the dog that gets to pee on everyone's tree.

The Five Eyes relationship is merely one element of the general relationship the U.S. has with most of the world's other nations. What we see is that the U.S. is to some extent partner and to some extent manager, and this ratio varies from nation to nation. Key elements of the U.S. military, intelligence, and financial structure are integrated into the structures of the client states. Some, like U.K., Canada, Australia, Israel, Japan, Saudi Arabia, and Germany, rank higher than other nations and in certain instances function as genuine partners. Others, such as Poland, Mexico, Chile, or Greece, rank lower on the hierarchy and serve other purposes (in the case of Greece, unfortunately, it is to be plundered at will and turned into an open air prison on the level of Palestine). Every nation has its role to play.

Ultimately, however, if a nation's key military systems are integrated with those of the U.S., it would be difficult for its leaders to pursue much of an independent policy. This is why NATO or EU nations are extremely unlikely to jump ahead of the U.S. on the matter of UFO disclosure.

There is another way to understand how America's military infrastructure dominates the international UFO coverup. According to 2015 statistics, the United States spends roughly 36% of the global military budget, far ahead of all other nations. In second place is China at (a rapidly rising) 13%. Saudi Arabia is third at 5%. Russia comes in next at 4%, followed by the United Kingdom at 3%.[18]

Of all the nations with significant military budgets, Russia and China are the only two that are outside the U.S.-dominated

---

[18] List of countries by military expenditures, From Wikipedia, the free encyclopedia.

2015 World Military Spending— 1,676.0 (in US dollars)	
1–United States (596.0)	11–Brazil (24.6)
2–China (215.0)	12–Italy (23.8)
3–Saudi Arabia (87.2)	13–Australia (23.6)
4–Russia (66.4)	14–United Arab Emirates (22.8)
5–United Kingdom (55.5)	15–Israel (16.1)
6–India (51.3)	16–Turkey (15.2)
7–France (50.9)	17–Canada (15.0)
8–Japan (40.9)	18–Spain (14.1)
9–Germany (39.4)	19–Iraq (13.1)
10–South Korea (36.4)	20–Poland (10.5)

system. All the others are integrated to some (usually a significant) extent into the U.S. command structure. Even more astonishing: when we look at the military spending of the U.S. and its various partners and dependencies, it works out to nearly 80% of all military spending in the world. Russia and China account for 17%, and a few others outside of the U.S. system (Iran, Syria, North Korea) make up a small remainder.

But even this does not fully explain the extent of American power over most of the world. Thanks again of some of the recent revelations, we now understand just how comprehensively the NSA spies on everyone. We learned, for instance, that the NSA completely monitored the cell phones of Brazilian President Dilma Rousseff and German Chancellor Angela Merkel. As well, naturally, as the cell phones (and emails and so on) of their ministers and staff. Imagine one of these national leaders—*any* national leader—planning to disclose the reality of UFOs ahead of the United States. Such a leader would have to be very careful, knowing full well that the NSA hears everything. Privacy is a relic of a bygone age, not for the 21st century. How would such a disclosure plan occur outside the U.S. decision-making structure? Would one use pencils and papers and whisper into each other's ears?

Incidentally, the NSA and CIA are leading candidates to have been behind the infamous "Wall Street coup" or "soft coup" against Dilma Rousseff in 2016. Rousseff was a classic Brazilian nationalist, who believed in a policy of economic independence from the U.S. and was a strong proponent of the BRICS alliance. Two years earlier, documents pertaining to the Brazilian government and its state run oil company, Petrobras, were mysteriously leaked to a judge hostile to the government, and a demonization campaign against Rousseff was promptly created, promoted by U.S. funded NGOs and Brazilian billionaires. Despite the lack of any corruption by Rousseff, she was finally impeached and deposed, allowing the IMF and Goldman Sachs once again to plunder the country. The rule here is, tangle with U.S. imperial interests at your peril.[19]

The threat of being deposed may not be as powerful as a more simple threat: blackmail. In a world where the NSA leaves no stone unturned and no important life left private, politicians around the world are very easily controlled. Russell Tice is the among the key NSA whistleblowers in American history. He was a key source in the 2005 *New York Times* report that exposed the Bush administration's use of warrantless wiretapping. Tice also stated that the NSA regularly spies on and *probably* blackmails leading political figures in the U.S. Other major intelligence community whistleblowers, including William Binney and Ray McGovern, have talked about this at length. McGovern expressed his opinion that President Barack Obama was afraid of being assassinated if he veered away from the dictates of the Deep State. McGovern heard an account from a "good friend" that when on one occasion Obama was accosted

---

[19] Wall Street Behind Brazil Coup d'Etat. The Impeachment of Dilma Rousseff, By Prof Michel Chossudovsky, Global Research, Sep 01, 2016.

by a progressive supporter who was disappointed at his failure to follow through on his campaign promises of reform, the President was said to have turned sharply and replied, "Don't you remember what happened to Martin Luther King Jr.?"[20]

The CIA and NSA have a totalitarian grip over the United States, but of course they engage in the same activities against leaders around the world. Threats and blackmail are surely an important reason that other nations don't give up the UFO secret. Go off road, off script, and you will be destroyed.

Another reason is bribery, one of the great unspoken realities of the political world. People are bought off all the time; it's simply the price of doing business. Money can make nearly anything right.

Bribery, blackmail, and threats of regime change. The carrot and stick combination is enough to keep most people in line.

There is yet another reason that most nations do not dream or dare of jumping ahead of the U.S. in UFO disclosure. Ultimately, the vast majority of them lack the data. Recall that twenty nations, account for 85% of global military spending. That means roughly 180 nations account for a mere 15%. These top level nations are the ones that we can safely assume have a technological infrastructure to manage such an intensely classified subject with any real knowledge and sophistication. We are talking about probably not much more than twenty nations that have the capability to "disclose" much of anything.

There is, in my view, one final reason most rations don't disclose ahead of the U.S. It is fear.

Not simply fear of what the U.S. would do to them if they got

---

[20] NSA Whistleblower: NSA Spying On – and Blackmailing – Top Government Officials and Military Officers. Posted on June 20, 2013 by WashingtonsBlog

out of line, but fear in general of this great unknown. The U.S. secret keepers have a fear, the Russians have a fear, and the Chinese have a fear. Everyone who has studied this phenomenon has concluded that it is utterly revolutionary.

Russia and China

So what of Russia and China? I am no expert in the internal dynamics of either nation, especially of China, but there are certain facts that are readily available. In the first place, there is the obvious reality that neither of these countries are under U.S. domination. That is a problem for them, because ever since the end of the Cold War, the U.S. national security strategy has been to pursue global hegemony—world domination in all but name. Of all nations on Earth, Russia and China stand in the way of that dream. As a result, western propaganda against both of them, especially Russia, began on a steady crescendo over the past several years, reaching a fever pitch during the Presidential election of 2016.

The U.S. national security establishment would like nothing more than to implement regime change on Vladimir Putin. In Russia during the 1990s, during the heyday of the vodka-fueled presidency of Boris Yeltsin, the entire nation was available to western banks and corporations at firesale prices. Naturally, the U.S. was pleased with that situation. Starting in 1999, Putin changed that policy and thereby incurred the enmity of the West. It is also clear that China's Xi Jinping is similarly too independent for Washington's taste.

It's fascinating and disturbing to see how the anti-Russian messaging has exploded. The coordinated media and political attacks took off in earnest after the western destruction of Libya in 2011. Once one of Africa's most prosperous and secular nations, western governments reduced Libya to its current status as a smoking jihadist-dominated ruin. Putin recognized the veneer of lies that covered the true motive of Libya's destruction (to prevent the introduction of a gold-based currency) and was furious. This started him on a path to do something revolutionary: defy the United States in the realm of global affairs. First in 2013, when he negotiated a settlement that prevented the U.S. from an air campaign against the government of Syria, then by supporting the decision of the people of Crimea to return to Russia following the U.S.-coordinated coup in Ukraine in 2014, and finally, perhaps most egregiously, by providing Russian military support at the request of the Syrian government in 2015 to combat the U.S.-backed jihadists (deceptively labeled in the west as "moderate rebels") that had overrun most of that country. As a result of these unforgivable transgressions, the western media labeled him as the new Hitler—a designation since handed over to Donald Trump.

The anti-Russia and anti-Putin campaign went into its highest gear during the summer and fall of 2016, all because of a brilliant deflection maneuver by the Hillary Clinton campaign. After Wikileaks released thousands of emails implicating corporate bias and corruption in the Democratic National Committee—bias that explicitly favored Clinton over her Democratic Party rival and populist-oriented Bernie Sanders—the Clinton campaign did something breathtaking. Using evidence-free assertions, the DNC spun the story away from its own corruption and blamed the leak on the Russians. Putin and the Russians "hacked" us, the DNC claimed. The western media enthusiastically went along for the ride, treating the world to one of the most astonishing political spectacles seen in years. Normally, anti-Russian hysteria is the job of the American Right, but for the first time in history, the American Left went into anti-Russian crazyland, implying and at times even accusing Donald Trump of being under the control, somehow, of the Russians. The American Left was brought to this incredible state of affairs with the support of the U.S. intelligence community and Deep State apparatus, which had its own reasons for opposing Trump. More on this later.

Back to Russia, which has its own long history of UFO encounters. Many of these were every bit as dramatic and incredible as have been experienced in the United States and elsewhere, and many involved that nation's military. There have also been retrievals of UFOs that have either crashed or otherwise come down. We learned about many of these events during the breakup period of Soviet Union—that is, the late 1980s and early 1990s. During that chaotic period, many government UFO files came to light, including files of the KGB. There were also a number of statements made by government officials. Several that seem very persuasive, and as for the individuals pictured here, all have made confirmed statements about the reality of UFOs.

Dimitri Medvedev, the number two politician in Russia next to Putin, made a provocative statement about extraterrestrials living in Russia in an interview from 2012. Pavel Popovich, the famous cosmonaut and Soviet Hero talked very openly many times about the UFO reality. Several prominent officials toward the end of the Soviet era also made startlingly blunt statements about UFOs. The late 1980s and early 1990s were a unique moment in Russian and Soviet history. Gorbachev was in power, everything was in flux, and people were talking. For

Dimitri Medvedev   Pavel Popovich   Igor Maltsev   Ivan Tretyak

instance, General Igor Maltsev and Senior Defense official Ivan Tretyak, two high ranking officials from that time, were very candid about the UFO phenomenon over Soviet skies. In 1990, Maltsev spoke at length about the extraordinary nature of a UFO encounter near Moscow during which Russian interceptors attempted to deal with this object—except that the object then turned around and began chasing the interceptor. The event was seen by hundreds of witnesses, including military personnel. Photographs were taken which have never been seen. Maltsev noted that the object performed S-maneuvers horizontally and vertically, an amazing capability. He added that there was no known technology that could do this, and that somehow the operators had "come to terms with gravity."[21]

The best thing American skeptics can do with statements like that is to call it Russian propaganda. But the evidence for the Moscow UFO sighting of March 1990 is overwhelming. Russia has had its UFO encounters, and has developed its own infrastructure to deal with this. Indeed, we have confirmation of sorts about this from the Condign report, created by British intelligence in 2000, noted earlier.

China is a greater challenge to understand, and less is known to western researchers. After Mao Zedong died in 1976, China

---

[21] "Multiple Witness Case at Russian Missile Base," at ufoevidence.org

experienced a relative openness about UFOs. One researcher in particular, Paul Dong, did a great deal of work exposing Chinese UFO cases. To this day there is an active Chinese UFO research community. Unfortunately, there is all too little communication with the West and still not much is known about the findings there.

I had the pleasure of meeting Dr. Sun Shi Li, one of the best-known Chinese UFO researchers, in 2013. Li had been the Spanish translator for Mao during the 1970s. A few years ago, Li was interviewed by Alejandro Rojas of Open Minds, based out of Phoenix. He spoke no English, but was translated from the Spanish by researcher Antonio Hunneus. The process at times seemed a bit convoluted, but it worked well enough. Unfortunately, very little tangible information came out.

Li mentioned, not surprisingly, that China experiences a great deal of UFO activity. Without giving much in the way of detail, he discussed a dramatic UFO incident on the northern border in 1999 that greatly concerned the authorities. He also seemed to believe there was a Chinese retrieval of a crashed UFO in 1951. He had little else to say about this possible event, and reported it only as inside rumor. China's infrastructure in 1951 was primitive, but if this rumor is true then China would have been deep into the UFO phenomenon fairly early on. Li wasn't even sure whether or not the Chinese military viewed UFOs as a threat.

Clearly, western researchers need to reach out more to the Chinese. Since China does have a strong UFO research commu-nity, this should be entirely feasible. There is an intriguing account about Chinese ufology from the 1990s told by C.B. Scott Jones, former Navy pilot and longtime aide to the power-ful U.S. Senator Claiborne Pell (D-RI), who for many years of Chairman of the Senate Foreign Relations Committee. Jones and Pell both had a longstanding interest in UFOs, and Jones on many occasions traveled to China, in part to gather information on the state of Chinese ufology for Pell. Jones was extremely impressed by the quality of the personnel involved and the information they obtained. In 2004 he said to journalist Linda Moulton Howe:

> The Chinese, when they told me, over and over again, of the amount of evidence that they have from which they conclude the ET phenomena is real, in the sense that they are real, tangible craft penetrating their airspace—that that issue is essentially settled with them. And I said 'Well, this being the case, why don't you make a public announcement—tell the world about this reality?' And there was a short embarrassed silence and he said, 'China will be a quick second after the United States announcement.' [22]

In 2006, speaking at a conference in Hawaii, Jones had this to say.

> The Chinese and the Russian have told me that they have recovered hardware. The Chinese have told me that when the U.S. makes an announcement, they will be a quick second. I have pondered that statement for years. Why would China defer to the U.S.? It implies that the U.S. has a leading role to play in disclosure. Why? [23]

Clearly Russia and China both experience UFOs, and both consider the phenomenon to be important.

It should also come as no surprise that, like the United States, neither would be especially interested in any form of disclosure in the near future. In the first place, there is the energy problem. It has been my opinion for some time that any form of UFO-

---

[22] Government Whistleblower C. B. Scott Jones on UFO Secrecy An interview by Linda Moulton Howe. *Nexus New Times Magazine*, Sep 2004, pp. 63-66.

[23] Options for a Planet in Peril, C.B. Scott Jones, Ph.D., Presented at the Extraterrestrial Civilizations and World Peace Conference Sponsored by the Exopolitics Institute, Kailua-Kona Hawaii, 11 June, 2006. expoliticsjournal.com

related disclosure would affect our global energy paradigm. The energy behind these objects is surely not petroleum-based, and any disclosure of the UFO reality implies a post-petroleum world. Russia and China would both be deeply affected, or more accurately the infrastructures and power structures of both would be affected. Russia's economy hinges on the sale of its oil and natural gas. No doubt both nations are researching non-hydrocarbon based energy possibilities. But, just like the rest of the world, they have infrastructures that would be seriously jolted once there was an acknowledgment that something better can replace our global addiction to oil.

Disclosure would be just as disruptive for China and Russia as it would be for any of the western nations. I see much hesitation, particularly for someone like Vladimir Putin, who is an extremely careful diplomat. The U.S. certainly accuses him of all kinds of activities and plans, few if any being true. The same applies to Xi Jinping. China may be assertive in its foreign policy, but it is not especially rash or reckless. Neither of these nations seek radical or revolutionary developments in global or domestic policy. It would seem to me that such qualities mitigate against a disclosure about UFOs.

- oil and gas key elements of Russian and Chinese infrastructures.

- power elites would face disruption.

- could the secret be used in the political chess game?

- to what extent are Russia and China truly independent?

Vladimir Putin and Xi Jinping

One supposes there would be a possibility of disclosure by Russia. Perhaps, as a result of the not-so-secret war being waged against Russia by the U.S. Deep State, that somehow Putin feels himself pushed to the wall. Would he do something dramatic? Would he release information that might damage the standing of the United States? Would he allow for the release of an important UFO secret? I can only speculate, but would think he would be more inclined to allow the release of something about 9/11. To my mind this would have a more controlled impact while still being disruptive to the United States. But ultimately I cannot speculate on this any better than the next analyst. I see Russia and China as wildcards. Although both have western factions within their political structure, both remain free of U.S. control and are therefore harder to predict.

During the summer of 2016, I realized that I would prefer that Russia or China break the UFO disclosure, rather than leave it to the United States. While being interviewed on this subject, I was asked whether I thought that President Obama would choose to make a UFO disclosure as part of his legacy, and to beat out the Russians or Chinese. At that moment, I realized that a Russian or Chinese disclosure would have the likelihood of being a more positive event for the world than would an American one. America, sadly, has betrayed itself. Once standing for the principle of freedom and self-determination of nations, it has morphed over several generations into a nation that seeks domination over all others. For the United States now to lead the disclosure process would be like Darth Vader leading it. The process would be filled with lies, spin, and propaganda, and probably only something bad would be the result.

People sometimes talk about the so-called Project Blue Beam, the alleged alien invasion false flag. For my part, I have always considered Blue Beam sheer fantasy. However, I can easily see disclosure itself as a type of false flag. A psych job on the rest of us to finalize a global totalitarian state. More on this later.

The Geopolitical Situation

UFOs are a key unspoken component to the global geopolitical situation, but it is still a piece within a larger puzzle. That larger puzzle has everything to do with global control. There is a global elite, and it has a simple plan: own everything. All the water, all the minerals, all the genetically modified foods that they will patent and force you and your grandchildren to consume forever. All of what were once publicly owned services, everything from schools to airports. One of their tools to accomplish this are the plethora of transnational trade agreements (one of which, the Trans Pacific Partnership, was quashed in early 2017). Most of these have been covertly negotiated and very quietly been put into place. Supporting this new world order of total financial control will be one of police state and surveillance control. Everyone with eyes can see this, and it is happening everywhere. It is not merely in the U.S. and Canada, but in Europe, in South America, and of course in Africa and most of Asia—regions that have always been oppressed by unfair social conditions.

Within the U.S., the middle class has been severely weakened. I live in the city of Rochester, New York, and I've seen the process going for the past 25 years. I watched Eastman Kodak go poof. Part of this was because Kodak failed to keep up in the digital age, but Kodak's demise is part of a larger trend. Globalization, from NAFTA onward, has contributed to the severe weakening of the middle class. Today, thirty eight percent of Americans make less than $20,000 a year. That is

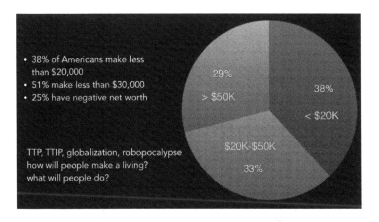

- 38% of Americans make less than $20,000
- 51% make less than $30,000
- 25% have negative net worth

TTP, TTIP, globalization, robopocalypse
how will people make a living?
what will people do?

29% > $50K

38% < $20K

$20K-$50K 33%

not a lot of money.

If we look into the future, beyond current globalization, we see what has been termed the robopocalypse. The Terminator is coming, but he isn't here to kill you. He just wants your job. Automation is believed to be unstoppable and many jobs will be lost. Undoubtedly some will be created, but will it be enough? Already our world has a high level of structural unemployment. How will people survive in the future? One thing is certain: unemployment and hopelessness mean an increasingly unstable and restive population.

Analyzing patterns of wealth, as opposed to income, is even more alarming. People talk about the One Percent, but we are better served by analyzing the top 10% of the One Percent. As of 2014, this .01% owned 22% of all U.S. national wealth in the United States. In a room of 100 people, if the total amount of wealth for everyone equaled $100, one person would own 42 of those dollars. But if that person could be divided into ten parts, one part would own 22 of those dollars. That is America today, and fundamentally it is the pattern around the world. Of course, we are talking about much more than money, because money buys power and influence. Our world has a political system, a media system, an economy, and so many other institutions that enable it to function. We are obligated to ask a simple question: who is in the best position to manipulate those institutions? It is a question that answers itself.

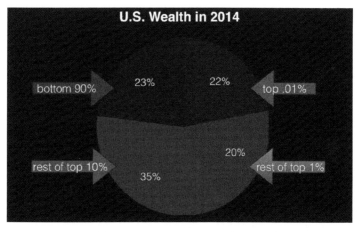

Within such a context of global theft and impoverishment, what kind of world are we headed toward? Clearly, a police state of some sort.

Recall Seattle in 1999. Unfortunately I believe this is not simply in our past, but our future. Indeed, anti-globalist scenes like what happened in Seattle happen nearly every week. Not usually as dramatic as Seattle, but they are out there, just seldom reported. In Seattle, demonstrators protested against the convening of the World Trade Organization (WTO), which was once again preparing to initiate a new round of pernicious neoliberal trade policies that even then was sucking the wind out of the American economy. Incredibly, the protesters, not less than 40,000 strong, shut the city down. They actually prevented attendees from entering the building, significantly hampering the WTO proceedings. Teargas did not work, nor did pepper spray.

Seattle, 1999.

Of course, a year and a half later came 9/11. The hammer came down, and suddenly people learned to duck their heads and not speak out. Because now if you protest, your face is photographed and entered into a database with facial recognition software. People learn to live in a world of surveillance and intimidation.

Presiding over that world of surveillance and intimidation is the global royalty, seeking to formalize its breakaway status from the world, legally, financially, and in every other way. I think of the breakaway civilization as based on more than technology. That is how I originally conceived the idea—as a radically advanced and covert technologically advanced society. I now see that society as having broken away in terms of money, of nations, and of the laws that most people have to follow.

We are moving toward the end of nations as we understand it. Entire nations are being plundered and turned over to banks, Greece being the most obvious current example. Recent cases of blatant western destruction of nations also includes Ukraine,

Syria, Libya, Yemen, and of course Iraq. American have never understood what happened in Syria because the U.S. policy from 2011 until 2017 had been to dismantle it. The same was true regarding Libya in 2011.

How is it that the U.S. can destroy entire nations and not have a national conversation about it? There will be a day when America is held accountable for this, if only in the pages of history.

This is the world we are moving into. An undeclared war by the United States, European Union, and NATO against all holdouts. Currently, this mainly includes the BRICS alliance, but also of course "renegade" nations like Iran, Syria, and North Korea.

The Globalists and UFOs

Throughout the ages, elites have entertained and practices unconventional esoteric beliefs that are unknown to the masses.[24] It appears that our current batch of handlers entertain ideas that are similarly off the map. Today there are rumors and claims that at least some of our elites are performing Satanic rituals and other awful things. We hear about the rituals of Bohemian Grove. The U.K. recently had scandals about pedophilia and satanism in its upper echelons. Such information leaks periodically. There is a dark side to what is going on at the top of our power structure, something that was depicted to some extent by Stanley Kubrick in his last film, *Eyes Wide Shut*. I have no doubt whatsoever that some of this behavior is encour-

---

[24] See Hall, Manly P. The Secret Teachings of All Ages (1928).

aged for purposes of blackmail.[25]

But do the elites also possess genuine esoteric knowledge that goes back through the centuries? As someone who has never been invited to their suarees, I cannot say. But I believe it is a reasonable estimate that at least some of them have access to secret, highly classified, and positively exotic technology. These individuals assuredly have some understanding of the implications of "others" visiting our world. What is their relationship to these others?

Once again, I don't know the answer to this question. Are they vassals? Are they secretly fighting the overlords like in a Hollywood movie? Did they happily sell us out?

I do believe that there are disclosure plans and possibilities. This is a secret that cannot be kept forever. Our society is in constant change. Whether in fifty years or fifty minutes, something will happen. Let us look at four possible candidates for UFO disclosure.

Disclosure Scenario #1: Fascist Disclosure

The first scenario disclosure I envision is what I call fascist disclosure. Sadly, I consider this the frontrunner of the four types. The people of this world are in a race against their elites. We have a few things going for us. For starters, we have the web, which for the last twenty years has revolutionized our consciousness and our ability to communicate with each other. We have social media, Skype, the Pirate Bay, and other amazing ways to share information. These are things that were unforeseen a mere generation ago. That gives us power.

---

[25] For example, see Kesel, Aaron. The Ultimate Exposure of Pedophile Rings in London, Hollywood, and More. Jul 7 2016.wearechange.org

From the point of view of the elites, that constitutes a problem, and the solution to that problem is to control the web. To turn it into TV, to commercialize it as much as possible, and to end net neutrality. This is a multi-pronged attack that has been continuing for as long as we have had the web.

High on the agenda is cracking down on the sharing of new ideas and technologies. One of my recurring fantasies is that some smart person, somewhere in the world, will develop a free energy device that will fit in the palm of your hand. Then they do the polite thing and upload the CAD version to the next generation of the Pirate Bay so that you can download it on your next generation 3-D printer and go off the grid. I see no reason why this cannot be possible. If it were to happen within the next ten years it would be a game changer in our world.

That is merely one breakthrough that can change the world. There are no doubt others, many that I cannot conceive of. But with new technology and new forms of communication, all possibilities exist. It is therefore a major policy of the elites to prevent disruptive breakthroughs from happening. They need to achieve complete control over the global system before the people can utilize any of these breakthroughs. This is why, in my view, there is a never-ending push to obtain these transnational agreements, since one of the key elements of all of them has to do with intellectual property rights, which of course would inhibit or even prevent the free sharing of breakthrough concepts. Especially so if the breakthroughs violate classified patents held in the black budget/breakaway world. In addition, we are also seeing a comprehensive global surveillance system going into place that will monitor all online activity.

The question remains: who will get to the finish line first? Will the people achieve a breakthrough disruption to the system, or will our elites clamp down for all time on that system, preventing unauthorized releases of information? I see this as the primary issue of our time.

Another problem, one I have discussed already, is that because of the ever-weakening of the middle classes everywhere, we see increasingly restive populations. These are people who are unhappy with how things are going. In the view of the elites, such people need to be controlled, but how? The answer is by creating a police state that monitors and intimidates them.

It also helps to divert and distract them with a full range of propaganda. In my forthcoming book on false flags, I have developed an analytical framework for the phenomenon which involves what I call the spectrum of propaganda.[26] This spectrum runs from the commonplace to the traumatic. It includes something as simple as the creation of specific cultural values to mold the minds of people, to more pernicious distractions in the form of junk culture and video games, to news media control, to covert operations and provocations, to regime change and finally various forms of false flags—which are simply the most intense form of propaganda. We are moving fast into a future world in which all forms of propaganda are systematically employed to manipulate and control the public. Many would say we are already there.

Looking further into the future, we see the prospect of a class-based transhumanism. It is inevitable that we will begin to see a synergy developing among the new technologies in the works: advance artificial intelligence, quantum computing, molecular computing, complete DNA control, implants for

---

[26] For those unfamiliar with false flags, they are events created by one agency (often an intelligence agency) that are blamed on another party, either a lone patsy or a group or nation.

superpowers, organic 3-D printing.

Consider what can develop from various combinations of the above technologies. Conceivably, if you can afford superhealth, superlongevity, superstrength, and superintelligence for your descendants, that could constitute some sort of utopia. If you cannot afford it, perhaps it would turn into a nightmare.

Such a state of affairs appears to be the inevitable end game. For those who stand to benefit from it, the prospect of complete dominance over the planet with the possibility of transhuman hyperdominance would be considered more important than any other goal, by far. Nothing, not UFO disclosure, nor anything else, would be allowed to stand in the way.

The problem with the UFO reality, however, is that its uncovering must be an inevitability. Human civilization is going through too many changes. There is simply too much instability. And so it could well be—in my view this is most likely—that a decision has been made that there must be no disclosure until the spin and control over the matter can be confidently achieved.

In other words, the plan would be for UFO disclosure to occur within a state of global fascism. Until then, there is simply no other motivation for any nation or any part of the international power structure to do it. Not until the entire international control system is fully achieved.

If or when such a thing occurs, then we might expect a rollout of the presence of these *others*, and even perhaps our clandestine black triangle fleet and who knows what else. Only when we are fully and completely encased within a 24/7 virtual fascist society will the authorities voluntarily offer their version of disclosure.

But the disclosure will not be truthful and certainly will not be complete. Consider that there are mountains of classified data that exist on this subject. It would be extremely easy for the managers of that data to take a sliver of that mountain—genuinely truthful information, but only a sliver—and to use that portion to promote a certain agenda. This seems most likely.

That is why I see disclosure as a potential false flag, in the sense of very selectively conveying certain information. The best way to keep a secret just might be to pretend to share it. Give up a little bit of it as a way to hide the greater truth, and perhaps keep the larger secret going for several more generations. The plan to keep the truth hidden must remain flexible to some extent. Plans, after all, must evolve to meet the changes of an continually changing society.

Disclosure Scenario #2: Premature Disclosure

Fascist disclosure might be the preferred plan of the secret keepers, but life is full of surprises. Disclosure might come by accident. When I wrote *A.D., After Disclosure* in 2010, the premise was that although there was no foreseeable motivation for the secret to come out, the forces in our world are such that we should expect the unexpected. I feel this remains a valid position.

Premature disclosure would be a messy and probably dangerous process. It could happen from an unexpected sighting, something undeniable and recorded by multiple sources, for instance. Or it could be a credible leak, perhaps from WikiLeaks. Or a surprise leak from another country such as Russia, China, or even a U.S. ally.

One trigger for premature disclosure could be an unraveling of U.S. geopolitical or global financial strategy. There are many sources of instability in our world. If the U.S. imposed petrodollar system should fall by the wayside—something that is slowly happening—there is a likelihood of a major economic correction that would strike like an earthquake in the U.S.[27] Or, it could simply be the ruinous policy of endless warfare coming home to roost in the form of wrecked infrastructure and economic deprivation at home and abroad. Or a new war that simply goes very, very wrong. Such events would cause powerful political forces to be unleashed. In such a situation, there would be many unhappy people, and that is precisely when major leaks can occur. This is what happened to the Soviet Union at the end of the 1980s, when that society began to unravel. Within the U.S. as of 2017, we already see an intelligence community that has already gone into "leak mode." This was made much easier by Barack Obama who, just before he left the White House, radically expanded the power of the infamous executive order #12333 (known as "twelve triple-three") which serves as the authorization for the NSA's most massive domestic spying programs. Obama's order allows the NSA seamlessly to share sensitive data on U.S. citizens with Washington's other 16 intelligence agencies.[28] With so much more readily accessible, more will come out. This potential will only increase as political and economic crises worsen. If "the UFO leak" were to occur in this environment, it might be impossible for the U.S. government to contain it.

Even so, we would have to expect that disclosure would be as self-serving as possible. The Washington spin machine would work in overdrive to manage the situation—led undoubtedly by

---

[27] A very good overview of the petrodollar system is "Preparing for the Collapse of the Petrodollar System" by Jerry Robinson in four parts at ftmdaily.com

[28] Emmons, Alex, Obama Opens NSA's Vast Trove of Warrantless Data to Entire Intelligence Community, Just in Time for Trump. The Intercept, Jan 13, 2017.

close collusion between the national-security-deep-state and the loyal mainstream media led by the power trio of *CNN*, *New York Times*, and *Washington Post*. The effect of this spin would not be to disclose, but to divert. We can assume there is an array of contingency plans in place for such unexpected leaks or sightings.

The good news for us is that, despite these plans, the power structure would still be caught off guard, and there will be a genuine possibility of opening the narrative from the sanctioned spin doctors. There is a chance for people to become energized and angry about having been lied to for so long. Instead of Occupy Wall Street, we might see Occupy Area 51, Occupy Wright-Patterson, or Occupy Pine Gap. Of course, just as Occupy Wall Street was infiltrated by the intelligence community, so too people must expect the same to happen regarding any future social unrest.[29]

Yet, citizens will have the opportunity to engage this subject, to organize, and to demand truth. No one should expect this process to be easy, nor even to lead to satisfying answers. Unless a disclosure from the power structure includes an alien at a podium next to the President, people will continue to argue over what the truth is. Resolving the questions could take generations or centuries. We live in an age of faux objectivity, where we are led to believe that once the "facts" are obtained we will "know" the truth. Well, there are indeed facts, and there is a truth. But our ability to objectify reality, to pretend that we know things when we really don't, often lures people into thinking that full disclosure and access to the truth is just a leak

---

[29] Infiltration to Disrupt, Divide and Misdirect Is Widespread in Occupy, By Kevin Zeese and Margaret Flowers. In two parts. *Truthdig*. Feb 24, 2012.

away. Unfortunately, reality—and the human mind—is too complex for such simple formulas.

One thing we can expect from a premature disclosure, is that people's trust in their leaders will plummet even further. In the U.S., disclosure on UFOs will inevitably lead to many other questions. People would be angry. *You lied about UFOs*, they would say. *What else are you lying about? 9/11? JFK? Underground bases? Secret technology?* Where such lines of inquiry will end is beyond the reckoning of the most farsighted prognosticator.

Disclosure Scenario #3: Insider Disclosure

Another form of disclosure can be called *insider disclosure*. In some ways, it can be grouped together with the previously discussed premature disclosure. Still, there are enough distinguishing characteristics about it that it deserves special mention.

For years, prominent insiders around the world have been leaking information on UFOs, or at least discussing the subject in a startlingly open manner. As far back as the 1950s and 1960s, there were people in the U.S. like former CIA Director Roscoe Hillenkoetter and Navy Admiral Delmar Fahrney who openly discussed the serious nature of the phenomenon and how insiders were concerned about it. Their friend, retired Marine Corps Major Donald E. Keyhoe, the most important UFO writer of the 1950s, frequently received sensitive information from military circles relating to the reality of UFOs.

Officials from other nations have also at times been surprisingly candid. In 1974, the French Minister of Defense, Robert Galley, stated during a radio interview that the French gendarmerie had been studying UFOs for twenty years, and that the number of reliable reports of UFO landings was "very great," and that some of the reports were "pretty disturbing."[30] There have been equally open statements from other officials, including the Spanish General Carlos Castro Cavero gave an interview in 1976, stating, "I believe that UFOs are spaceships or extraterrestrial craft... The nations of the world are currently working together in the investigation of the UFO phenomenon. There is an international exchange of data...."[31]

Robert Galley and Carlos Castro Cavero:
two important whistleblowers of the 1970s.

In 1977, Japanese Major General Hideki Komura, advisor to the Cabinet Research Office in Japan (equivalent to Japan's CIA), stated that during the 1950s there were high level official Japanese UFO investigations based on the American Project Blue Book and cooperating closely with the United States government investigations. Quite a significant "disclosure," but then he discounted this, saying that the project collapsed because of the "garbage reports" being received alongside more credible data. One might wonder, why would an intelligence

[30] Timothy Good, Above Top Secret: The Worldwide UFO Cover-up (Quill, 1989), p. 129.

[31] George Filer, Filer's Files #49-2014, Dec 3 2014.

operation close down simply because not all the data it receives is valid?[32]

In more recent years, the Apollo 14 astronaut Edgar Mitchell, who died in early 2016, told me privately several times and also said publicly that he had two elite contacts who confirmed to him the existence of recovered alien technology and bodies. I have always considered this a particularly explosive claim, and yet, predictably, the mainstream media establishment persistently ignored his statements.[33]

Dr. Edgar Mitchell with the author, July 2004.

Within the U.S., there have been several times when, to those people paying attention, there were inside rumblings pressing for openness on the matter of UFOs. According to the Air Force Captain Edward Ruppelt, the head of Project Blue Book, it happened in 1952. That year saw a dramatic upsurge in UFO sightings by military personnel and civilians alike. According

---

[32] Spencer, John. The UFO Encyclopedia. Avon Books, 1991, p. 180.

[33] Waveney Ann Moore. "Astronaut: We've had visitors." St. Petersburg Times, Feb 18, 2004.

to Ruppelt, there was a definite faction within the military and classified world that believed telling the truth to the public was the best policy. Through the late 1950s and into the 1960s, the National Investigations Committee on Aerial Phenomena (NICAP) quietly cultivated relationships with members of Congress in order to hold open hearings on the matter. There were several times when NICAP's Director Donald Keyhoe thought it would happen. Each time their efforts came up short. When another significant upswing in sightings occurred during the mid-1960s, it became impossible to silence the matter. Even Michigan Congressman (and future President) Gerald Ford discussed it in the halls of Congress. Some people wondered, would it all come spilling out? In that case, the Air Force and CIA masterfully kept the initiative, and the so-called scientific investigation of UFOs, known as the Condon Committee, was the result: a scientific farce and public relations success that debunked the matter as far as the public knew.

But through the subsequent decades, efforts quietly continued that caused some to wonder if the ultimate leak might occur. In 1973, it appeared that some Air Force generals were going to facilitate leaks in the form of authentic video. According to researcher Grant Cameron, who looked into this matter extensively, the effort stalled when it appeared the Nixon presidency was not going to last.[34] During the early years of the internet, the late 1980s and early 1990s, new claims gained wide circulation, some seemingly plausible, others not so much. Even so, there did appear to be machinations afoot as high as the White House

---

[34] Greg Bishop, Project Beta: The Story of Paul Bennewitz, National Security, and the Creation of a Modern UFO Myth (Pocket Books, 2005) pp. 200-202. Also, Dr. Henry Azadehdel interviews Robert Emenegger. Written by Dr. Henry Azadehdel, 05 Mar 1990, at presidentialufo.com

of President George Bush to facilitate a genuine UFO disclosure. According to the sources on this, the main stumbling block was Secretary of Defense Dick Cheney.[35] Along these lines, I should add that in a conversation I had with a senior government official I have occasionally spoken to on the matter, I was told that UFO disclosure comes up in a serious way "every five years or so."

During the 1990s and into the 21st century, as the internet created a completely new world, ever greater numbers of people quietly entered the conversation about UFO secrecy. It is impossible to know how truthful or knowledgeable each person is on a case by case basis. But it is undeniable that high level government and military personnel have been talking to researchers, usually quietly. I myself have been on the receiving end of some of these communications. The problem all of the leakers have at this point is fear of professional repercussions. I was told this explicitly by a senior scientist with the appropriate connections and clearances, as well as by Edgar Mitchell. For instance, in 2006 I said to Dr. Mitchell that I realized that he might not be able to tell me the identity of the two high level individuals who confirmed to him the existence of deep black ET programs. But I asked him if he could give me any other information about them that would be useful to me as a researcher. His answer was that he could not. The people who came to him, he said, did so at great risk, professionally, personally, and to their families. While they were living, he said, he would not reveal their identities.

I don't know if Mitchell included Vice Admiral Thomas R. Wilson as one of this sources. But I learned that Mitchell and

---

[35] Dolan, Richard M. UFOs and the National Security State: The Cover-Up Exposed, 1973-1991, Keyhole Publishing Co., 2009) p. 565

Dr. Steven Greer met with Wilson in 1997, while Wilson was head of intelligence for the Joint Chiefs of Staff (a position designated as J2). I learned from a source who had access to what had happened, and who had a transcript of Wilson later privately discussing the meeting with someone. Mitchell and Greer met with Wilson in April 1997 as part of Greer's early disclosure initiative. They were able to get a meeting with Wilson due to Mitchell's stature. They provided information about the rogue nature of the black budget programs connected to the UFO/ET phenomenon. They gave Wilson enough information that he followed up and found at least one of the programs. Or rather, they found Wilson. Lawyers for the program grilled him, wanting to know how he learned about its existence. He did learn that technology "not made by human hands" was being studied.

As an aside, I learned about this meeting before Greer outed Wilson by name in his book *Hidden Truth, Forbidden Knowledge*. Prior to that I only knew that a sensitive meeting had taken place with Greer, Mitchell, and a prominent insider. When I learned it was Wilson, I found him and arranged an interview in early 2007. In the only instance in my life when I posed as someone I wasn't, I told him I was an admirer of his career and was doing research on his tenure at J2. He obligingly set up a time for a phone call. When we spoke by phone and I told him what I was actually calling about, his tone changed immediately and dramatically. When he pretended to have no recollection of any such meeting, I made it clear that I knew specifics of what transpired. He quickly raised his voice, admitted the meeting took place, but added that any of this stuff about him investigating UFOs was "poppycock" and ended the phone call.

What is important here, in the context of disclosure, is that the subject is clearly a sensitive one in certain circles. But it is not something that is covered in ordinary military-intelligence channels. Whoever is managing this secret is doing so outside the normal protocols we would expect. I say this because of yet another conversation I was fortunate to have with a very prominent and well-connected individual, formerly of the CIA. He is a well known person, at least in certain circles, and very brilliant. On one occasion he pointed out that not all Presidents are fully briefed on the subject. "Some have known more than others," he told me. The reason is that some are not considered reliable by the insiders, essentially those members of the deep state, to be trusted with the information.

On another occasion, during a long conversation, this man told me that in his retirement, he was able to have personal conversations about UFOs with 16 individuals who's government positions had either been U.S. President, CIA Director, Defense Secretary, or Defense Undersecretary. Their responses were instructive. "Three or four," he said, asked him why he was wasting his time with such nonsense. "Two or three" replied that they too had been briefed in some detail on the subject. All the rest—more than half—became very interested in learning everything he knew because they had not been able to get any good information. The clear inference is that at the pinnacle of the U.S. defense and intelligence establishment, the individuals one would expect to be the most plugged in were generally out of the loop. I asked this man, "so what are we talking about? Presumably some behind the scenes type of control group with all the power? Something like a Bilderberg subgroup?" His answer was "yes, that is my belief. Something like that."

Anytime any researcher, myself certainly included, talks to people of the CIA or the intelligence community, we have to be aware of the definite possibility that we are being manipulated in some manner. In my own limited dealings with such people, I acknowledge it is possible that they have tried to manipulate me. But I am not inclined to think this has been so in my case. The people I spoke to have mostly been fairly well known, and all would have something to lose if I exposed them. In my opinion, a certain level of mutual trust was formed that enabled the conversations to take place at all. My governing assumption continues to be that the information given to me was true as far as the individuals understood it.

That being so, then, any true insider leaks could be something of an attack on the power structure itself, unless of course the leakers sought to bring the President and his staff into the picture. In such a context, this makes the drama of 2016 rather interesting. This concerned rock star Tom DeLonge of the band Blink 182 and Hillary Clinton's Campaign Chair, John Podesta.

DeLonge has had a longtime interest in UFOs and through 2015 cultivated connections with several well placed insiders in the defense and aerospace fields. On January 25, 2016, he led a Google Hangout with Podesta and three other intriguing individuals on the subject of UFOs and the possession of alien technology.[36] One of these was Major General William N. McCasland, Commander of Wright-Patterson Research Laboratories and manager of the Air Force's $2.2 billion science and technology program. Another was retired USAF Major General Michael Carey. Carey was the Special Assistant to the Commander, Air Force Space Command, Peterson Air Force Base, which is also the home of NORAD. The other key person at

---

[36] Hillary campaign manager held UFO meeting with USAF generals, rock star and top secret aircraft developer. Posted by: Alejandro Rojas October 18, 2016 openminds.tv

DeLonge's Google Hangout with Podesta was Rob Weiss, Executive Vice President & General Manager Advanced Development Programs (Skunk Works) at Lockheed Martin Aeronautics.

It appears to be McCasland who told DeLonge that the military possess alien technology and bodies. The group apparently formulated a plan to achieve disclosure in conjunction with a Hillary Clinton presidency. As a result, DeLonge established a communication with Podesta, who has had a longstanding public interest in UFOs. The Google hangout these men had has been documented by Wikileaks. From what the record reveals, particularly the email correspondence in the aftermath of their video conference, it is not clear that Podesta was strongly committed to the disclosure process. If he was, it is not evident in the released documentation.

One might say the question is moot with the election of Donald Trump—to the shock of the political establishment around the world. However, perhaps not so moot. In early March 2017 DeLonge promised a major revelation of the UFO cover-up to be announced soon.[37] So perhaps the world will learn something important, or perhaps we will be disappointed.

Even so, the possibility of a disclosure process initiated and driven by concerned insiders should always be considered a possibility.

Throughout 2015 and 2016, when the collective voices of the power structure had already anointed Hillary Clinton as the presumptive next President, some people in the UFO field believed that she would be the Disclosure President. The logic

---

[37] Andrew Griffin, "Tom DeLonge is about to reveal an alien conspiracy, Blink-182 singer suggests after receiving UFO award." *Independent*, 2 March 2017.

behind a Clinton disclosure—or even an Obama disclosure—was promoted most heavily by Steven Bassett. His idea was that her connection to the Rockefeller initiative of the 1990s would force the issue open. This had been the effort of Laurence Rockefeller during the early years of the Bill Clinton presidency, when the billionaire attempted using his personal influence to encourage a public admission of the UFO reality. It is certainly true that Hillary Clinton met with Rockefeller during this time, and was photographed with him at his ranch in Jackson Hole, Wyoming. She was even carrying a book by the astronomer Paul Davies entitled *Are We Alone?*

For over twenty years, the mainstream media refused to touch the issue, despite the fact that it's clearly fascinating, and that millions of people would certainly be interested in knowing about it. Bassett believed that by publicizing her connection to the Rockefeller initiative, it would spark a media campaign to get to the bottom of her interest in this subject. He even speculated that Obama might himself disclose prior to a Hillary

Hillary Clinton with billionaire Laurence Rockefeller.

Clinton presidency as a way to strengthen his own legacy.

I will say again, as I said throughout 2015 and 2016, that I never believed in a Hillary Clinton disclosure event, nor in a Barack Obama disclosure. Nor did I believe in the absurd claims of an Obama disclosure promoted by other people with alleged "inside" sources as early as 2009 and 2010. As I have tried to make clear, such pronouncements would be political insanity in the extreme. The people making such predictions in 2009 knew nothing about geopolitics, nor about the revolutionary implications of disclosure. Something we can be quite assured a seasoned political operative like John Podesta knows full well.

That being said, we might ask why Podesta offered his famous tweet in 2015 expressing his great disappointment at the world once again not achieving #disclosure. The obvious question is, why in the world would Podesta make such an incredibly naive tweet? It's one thing for an outsider idealist who believes in such things as truth in human civilization to want disclosure. But for one of the most savvy political operators in the U.S. to say it is something else entirely. Why would he say such a thing?

John Podesta
@Podesta44
Follow

1. Finally, my biggest failure of 2014: Once again not securing the #disclosure of the UFO files.
#thetruthisstilloutthere cc: @NYTimesDowd

8:55 AM - 13 Feb 2015

1,221 RETWEETS 699 FAVORITES

Not knowing Mr. Podesta, I cannot presume to answer. But I simply cannot take his statement seriously, and certainly not at face value. I have no reason to think he isn't sincere when he says he is interested in the UFO phenomenon. Indeed, he has continued to tweet about matters related to extraterrestrial life. But one must also consider that in saying what he did, he demonstrated an astute insight: that 2016 was not 1996. In other words, twenty years of the web and social media have changed culture dramatically enough that the UFO subject is now out of the bottle, and it's not going back in. People talk about UFOs, they see the topic of aliens and space being portrayed in movies and television shows all the time. UFOs have become a brand, and as such they have their own market. Podesta was the first major political power player to appreciate that there is a "UFO vote." Not as a primary issue for many people, but as something cool, as interesting, and if handled properly, not too nutty. This is my own assessment of Podesta's interest in UFOs, and would explain why he encouraged the media at times actively to ask Hillary Clinton about UFOs. It also explains why he did not appear especially engaged in moving ahead on disclosure plans with DeLonge following their video conference. Granted, Podesta was extremely busy running Hillary Clinton's campaign, but if this were a truly important issue for him, we might have expected to see more genuine enthusiasm for the project.

Hillary Clinton and John Podesta have been closely connected to Goldman Sachs and the financial elites that own the world. They made their political fortune as the active managers for the true owners of our world. Those owners certainly must recognize UFO disclosure as the ultimate disruptor of the world order. Podesta and the Clintons might be many things—both, after all have actively promoted the lie of the "Russian hack" of the U.S. Presidential election—but they are not fools, and they are certainly not idealists.[38]

Disclosure Scenario #4: People Driven Disclosure

The fourth disclosure scenario I envision is what I call people driven disclosure. This is the one I personally believe in, and I think would offer the greatest opportunities for positive change. It is difficult for most of us to imagine changing grand politics. We can, however, change culture, and in many ways this is what ultimately drives political change. When the culture changes, so do the politics.

I have often considered gay marriage as an interesting model for how change can work in the UFO arena. A little more than a century ago, Oscar Wilde sat in a British prison for his so-called abomination. As recently as the 1990s, despite the great strides in the overall acceptance of homosexuality, gay marriage was still unthinkable in the U.S., as well as most of the

---

[38] One of many intelligent analyses of the lie of the Russian hack is by Joe Clifford, "Russian Hacking: The CIA Never Lies?" at Global Research, Dec 23, 2016.

world. All leading politicians spoke against it. How then did we get to a situation of such dramatic and rapid change?

It happened because of the cultural work that had previously been done. During the course of the twentieth century, especially from the 1950s onward, it was the bravery of selected individuals who came out openly, who had to confront entrenched viewpoints and intense hostility. Today, it is difficult for most people to appreciate that hostility without having lived through it, or at least studying the history. But over the generations, attitudes evolve. By the 21st century, the cultural foundation was prepared. Then, like a tidal wave, gay marriage went from something that was unheard of to something that has become common and uncontroversial.

That is the power of cultural transformation. Regarding the UFO subject, I believe a similar transformation is at work. This was the true power of the Citizen's Hearing on Disclosure of 2013, organized by Steven Bassett. This was a week-long event at the National Press Club in Washington, where forty researchers and insiders presented testimony to six retired members of the U.S. Congress and Senate. The real impact of the Hearing was not in creating immediate political change, although that might have been the goal of some people. Its power was in its afterlife on Youtube, where million of people searching for information on UFOs found articulate, serious, and concise treatments of the subject before a serious-minded panel of retired members of Congress. That is one way to change the culture.

The other way, ultimately more powerful still, is by individual people with an interest in this subject to be brave. To be fearless in talking about it with family, friends, and colleagues. For many years, to many people, UFOs have not seemed a safe topic to discuss openly. Generations of media ridicule have inhibited people from wanting to talk about it, despite the natural interest that anyone with an inquiring mind would have about it. When people talk about anything in a candid, open, and dispassionate manner, it opens the door for many more. Suddenly those people realize that it's not a dangerous subject. It's a fascinating subject that opens countless intellectual doors. They discover that they have had a hunger they never knew existed. They wake up.

There is no question in my mind that such a change is happening. Over the quarter century that I have been studying UFOs, I have seen the change. We are not where we were in the 1990s.

Part of this change is reflected in the growth of what we can call the Disclosure Movement. Perhaps calling it a movement is a bit generous. Those few individuals who have promoted the idea have not created a bonafide organization. Like most of the researchers in the UFO field, disclosure advocates have been scraping by for two decades. The movement has also attracted more than its fair share of self-appointed gurus, with several people who are clearly psychologically unhinged. Shortcomings aside, the movement has made genuine contributions to the cause of truth. Even Steven Greer's famous Disclosure Press Conference of May 2001, marred by a messianic certainty about the nature of these other beings—and a deeply politically naive platform of "banning" space based weapons—presented several government insiders and UFO witnesses that could have made a difference in our public discourse, had the mainstream media covered them with anything approaching fairness.

Similarly, the multiple X-Conferences in Washington D.C. organized by Steven Bassett between 2004 and 2010 had a positive impact on opening the discussion about government UFO secrecy, despite the shamefully negative coverage by the

Washington Post and other mainstream outlets. I was proud to have presented at every one of them, as well as at the Citizen's Hearing on Disclosure, which I mentioned a moment ago.

Other events and press conferences, most notably one organized in 2007 by filmmaker James Fox and journalist Leslie Kean, and another in 2010 by researcher Robert Hastings, carefully presented important facts from military and political insiders that were deserving of far better coverage then they received.

These events are a signal that the mood is changing, things are happening, despite the intransigence of the mainstream media—and the occasionally absurd naysayers within the UFO research community itself.

The conferences are only a part of the cultural change we are seeing. The point is that people take the initiative on this matter. I am not interested in a disclosure that includes a global police state. I would rather opt out altogether and take a rocketship to Mars, because I certainly would not want to live here. As interested as I am in gaining an open confirmation of the UFO reality, I would rather have my freedom. Disclosure is valuable because it enables the people to reclaim their political power and freedom. In her excellent book, *The Shock Doctrine*, Naomi Klein discussed the phenomenon of learned helplessness. You can shock rats randomly and take away their ability to protect themselves—as a result they stop trying. They give up and become helpless. They become depressed and listless.[39]

This also happens to people. When we lose the power to run our lives, when we know we are being lied to but don't know how to get to the truth, we develop a sense of helplessness and

---

[39] Klein Naomi. The Shock Doctrine: The Rise of Disaster Capitalism (Metropolitan Books, 2010).

hopelessness. Nothing is worse than this. Yet, by taking the initiative on this most important of public and societal issues, we can recover our power and, perhaps more importantly, our sense of agency and independence. We must be brave and willing to fight—not physically by causing harm, but in the realm of ideas. We can reclaim our power and unlearn the helplessness.

There are a number of ways we can do this. We can encourage and support those among us who publish good UFO data. We can meet other like-minded people through conferences and online connections. We can become informed and challenge ourselves. We can read good information on the subject that is reasoned and respects our intelligence.

We can also withdraw our support from the oppressive aspects of the dominant culture. It means opt out when you can. This can include many things, but it all comes down to maintaining an independent point of view from the mainstream. Recognize that the corporate news and entertainment system misleads and distracts you. If you are a football fan, recognize the manipulation and ritualistic pageantry of the Super Bowl half-time show. If you are a news hound, research and learn to identify the omission, spin, deception, and outright fakery of the mainstream news outlets. If you have children, you might consider the value of homeschooling them, something I did and remain proud of.

Talk to others about this subject. Be brave. I have found that when people discuss UFOs with others in an intelligent way that doesn't overreach, others are responsive. And if they aren't, so what? Most of us lack a proper understanding of ourselves, much less other people, so what does it matter if someone else decides to criticize you?

This is our life, our moment. Let us make the most of it.

Engage in what action you can, support others when that makes sense, and inspire others.

The Trump Era and Disclosure

I was as surprised as anyone by the victory of Donald Trump over Hillary Clinton in the 2016 U.S. presidential election. Like many other independent analysts, including Julian Assange, I had been certain that the establishment would not allow a Trump presidency to happen.

For sure, the power elite closed ranks and did everything possible to ensure a victory for Clinton. This included not only the Democratic party (which previously played dirty tricks against Bernie Sanders), but the entire mainstream media machine, the financial community, the European Union, and even the Republican party itself. If nothing else, I had concluded that the media alone had done a sufficient job of demonizing Trump with multiple negative headlines daily for more than a year so as to make him unelectable to the American people.

For more than a year, the world was told that Trump was a racist, sexist, xenophobe, liar, cheat, and narcissist. The attack bears all the marks of a coordinated effort among the major news outlets: *CNN*, *New York Times*, *Washington Post*, *Huffington Post*, *USA Today*, and the rest. It is starkly reminiscent of the concerted media attack against Brazil's Dilma Rousseff which culminated earlier in 2016 in her impeachment and removal from power. In the case of Rousseff, we see what has been alternately described as a soft coup or a Wall Street coup, rather along the lines of the "color revolutions" of a few years earlier (which are frequently CIA-NGO orchestrated). In both cases, pretexts were created and hammered home by an insistent media that whipped up public opinion. In Brazil, it worked. It seemed like it would work in the U.S.

It is important to understand why Trump was demonized. To be sure, his character made it easy. There is no shortage of narcissistic, sexist, or otherwise offensive statements in his repertoire from which to draw. But I have never and will never believe this is why he was demonized. Ultimately, Trump is a disruptor, and his disruption falls squarely against the two key pillars of the American ruling elite's ideology: neoliberalism and neoconservatism.

Unlike traditional liberalism and conservatism, neoliberalism and neoconservatism are not opposites. Neoliberalism is merely another name for transnational globalization, while neoconservatism is nothing other than the U.S.-dominated global empire project. They work together, two inhuman, anti-human processes that ensure a tiny minority of people control and own all the resources worth owning in this world. Hillary Clinton, as the ultimate representative of such an agenda, received unwavering support from all segments of that establishment, certainly from the media. Trump, on the other hand, was vilified.

This is because, at least in his rhetoric, Trump showed that he was not a reliable globalist or empire-builder. Whatever else one can say about him, he repeatedly spoke to hard-core Republican gatherings against the 2003 war in Iraq and the unconscionable destruction in 2011 of Libya. As an aside, I remain astonished at my self-described "progressive" friends who consistently overlook the obliteration of Libya, all based on lies and greed. The wreck of that nation will forever be a black stain on the careers of Obama and Clinton, and on the legacy of the United States as a whole.

For Trump to criticize these wars, as incompletely as he did, nevertheless took political courage and he was right to do so. He spoke out forthrightly against the perfidious TPP and TTIP, agreements which go far beyond free trade and truly hand over national and local rights to transnational corporations, seemingly for all time. Trump's position on this matter, it is worth noting, was essentially that of Ralph Nader, one of the leading left politicians in modern U.S. history, who has spoken about the perils of globalization for decades. To his credit, Trump also never signed on to the obscene anti-Russian hysteria promoted by Clinton and the entire national security establishment, whether from Democrats or insane members of the Republican party such as John McCain or Lindsey Graham. And, despite his obvious lack of deep understanding of the problems concerning Syria and the rest of the Middle East, Trump showed a willingness to work with the legitimate (and secular) government of Bashar al-Assad in fighting the jihadists that overran that country. It is true that rhetoric is one thing and action quite another, but Trump's rhetoric as a candidate placed him in a position diametrically opposed to everything the past several war-making presidencies have stood for. Hence his demonization.

That was Trump the candidate. Just two months into his presidency as of this writing, Trump has quickly found himself in the middle of a war with the national security community and major media—the deep state, to use the terminology of other analysts—that are clearly seeking to disable the least palatable elements of his program. It seems that the national security establishment spied on him as a candidate in what would appear to be a gross violation of law, and it is definitely clear that it leaked the contents of telephone calls of one of his closest advisors (Michael Flynn) in order to destroy him. Since it is early in his presidency as of this writing, where this will all lead is anyone's guess. It could well be that Trump has already been swallowed up by the national security apparatus and has continued the American tradition of warrior presidents. Within a month of his election, he engaged in needlessly hostile rhetoric with Russia, continued and expanded a brutal war against Yemen—one of the world's poorest nations—and sent several hundred new American troops to Syria, against the wishes of that nation's legitimate government. From this vantage point, his rhetoric as a candidate looks increasingly like a classic bait-and-switch, but only time will tell.

Nevertheless, there still appears to be a war going on around Trump, and this could have implications for the UFO secret. Trump does not appear to have made any public statements about the UFO subject. I don't know whether or not he takes it seriously. But we are in a new era, and talking about UFOs is not the kiss of death it once was. Moreover, Trump is clearly sympathetic to alternative media in general, which after all had a great deal to do with getting him elected. He is friendly with Alex Jones of Infowars, a man who has talked at length about 9/11 and other false flags on his show, and who even uses the term breakaway civilization. I would be shocked, frankly, if Trump were a skeptic on UFOs. As far as whether or not he has been briefed on UFOs since becoming President, I do know of any informed opinions.

But what if, during the course of Trump's war with the deep state, he gains access to a powerful secret and decides to use it as a weapon in his power struggle? If he were to learn an important truth about 9/11 or UFOs, would he reveal it? For all I know, Trump just might just do so. If Trump has any of the disruptor left in him after some time in the White House, he could easily be a greater threat to the established order than Hillary Clinton could ever have been. It is entirely possible that he might entertain the ultimate disruption of UFO disclosure. A small bit of irony, considering the stock that some people placed in a Hillary Clinton disclosure.

Although it is still unrealistic to expect UFO disclosure coming from the U.S. government any time soon, there are differences now with prior eras. We live in revolutionary times, technologically, socially, economically, and now politically. Our world is in flux, and within such a situation, things can happen unexpectedly. The Trump presidency was entirely unexpected, and placed the neolib-neocon establishment on the back foot for a brief moment. But it has never ceased in trying to regain the initiative.

The reality is that the U.S. is a global empire that is resisting the inevitable development of a multipolar world with all its might. That brings great danger, and there are many crazy people inside Washington who think they can stave off the inevitable. Those people had the ear of Bush, Obama, and the Clintons. They were and remain very dangerous. They are still in the U.S. government and are now increasingly gaining the ear of President Trump. The question of UFO disclosure is merely one of many treacherous issues that the coming four years will see play out. Personally, I am more concerned about a false flag designed to throw us into another major regional war, complete with all the fascist trappings it will bring.

Final Words

No matter what disclosure scenario transpires, do not expect utopia. Disclosure will not solve all of our problems. We are human beings, after all. We cannot solve all of our problems, because that is how we are. Remember when we were supposed to ascend in 2012? The entire ascension movement was nothing other than a mass cultural death wish. Our world is in such a bad state that people can easily despair of solving some of our problems and, in the case of the ascension belief, traipsed off into fantasyland. There is nothing wrong with having ideals and being an idealist. But utopias are the preserve of fools, and those who push them are either fools themselves or opportunistic manipulators of the hopelessly naive.

Any form of disclosure will be messy with questions that will remain unanswered for a long time. One simple reason is that it is highly unlikely that a disclosure event will be accompanied by a grey alien at the podium next to the President. The cultural wars, in other words, will continue. The evangelicals will argue with the tree hugging New Agers. There is no bridge long enough to connect those points of view. The scientific skeptics will have their own opinion on the matter.

Disclosure has great scientific implications, but is fundamentally a political process. Because we are living in an increasingly neofascist global political system, it would be ideal for disclosure to help break that neofascism. It should confront the breakaway black budget culture and financial criminality that has dominated our world.

Ultimately, disclosure will make public that there are *others* here with us. Coming to terms with that reality will take generations. To say nothing of whether or not we will ever be able to communicate directly, in the flesh, with these other beings. It is entirely possible that we will never be ready to deal with them. But being unready has seldom prevented a thing from happening. I was not ready for my first child, but it happened anyway. Life is a journey for which we are forever unprepared. Whether we think it's a good idea or a disaster, disclosure will happen. We like to believe we have control over things, but that is one of our illusions.

There are many other questions to ask. Do these other beings support our global status quo? Do they want to help us develop a higher consciousness or level of civilization, as some believe? Although no one can know the answer to this, we might wonder why there is no evidence they have helped us to create a better, more prosperous and just world? Perhaps they don't care very much either way. Perhaps we are in a situation where we are utterly outmatched.

If so, I will not despair. Our life is a beautiful gift that we will one day have to return. All lives end the same way: they end. Our job, as thinking, reasoning beings with the capacity to imagine, create, and love, is to journey through our life, and to encounter not only the occasional triumphs that we all seek, but to face the inevitable challenges and dark nights of the soul, and to embrace it all.

Above all, we should seek truth. Of all the pursuits that can be undertaken by free people, truth is the most noble, the most difficult, the most worthy. Along with love, it is what brings us closest to the gods, to whatever is divine that resides within us. And nobody has the power to deter us from that path.

About the Author

Richard Dolan is among the world's leading UFO researchers, historians, and publishers. He has written four groundbreaking books. These include two volumes of history, *UFOs and the National Security State*, an analysis of the future, *A.D. After Disclosure*, and *UFOs for the 21st Century Mind*, a fresh treatment of the entire subject. He has appeared widely on television, has lectured around the world, and is a frequent guest on radio shows such as *Coast-to-Coast AM*. Currently, he is the writer and host of the series *False Flags*, which is scheduled to appear on Gaia TV in 2017, and he is also writing a book on the same subject.

He also hosts two radio shows: *The Richard Dolan Show* on KGRA and *The Effed Files*, and is the publisher of Richard Dolan Press, which features the work of many leading thinkers exploring alternative realities in our world.

Find him at http://richarddolanpress.com.

By Richard Dolan Press

Richard M. Dolan, *Ufos for the 21ˢᵗ Century Mind: A Fresh Guide to an Ancient Mystery.*

Richard M. Dolan, *Ufos and the National Security State: The Cover-Up Exposed, 1973-1991.*

Richard M. Dolan. *The Secret Space Program and Breakaway Civilization.*

Grant Cameron and T. Scott Crain, Jr. *UFOs, Area 51, and Government Informants: A Report on Government Involvement in UFO Crash Retrievals.*

Mike Clelland, *The Messengers: Owls, Synchronicity, and the UFO Abductee.*

Chuck Harrison, *Recovery: A Novel*

Chase Kloetkze with Richard M. Dolan. *Admissible: The Field Manual for Investigating UFOs, Paranormal Activity, and Strange Creatures.*

Eve Lorgen. *The Dark Side of Cupid: Love Affairs, the Supernatural and Energy Vampirism.*

Bruce Maccabee, Ph.D. *The FBI-CIA-UFO Connection: The Hidden UFO Activities of USA Intelligence Agencies*

Bruce Maccabee, Ph.D. *Abduction in My Family: A Novel of Alien Encounters.*

Philip Mantle. *Once Upon A Missing Time: A Novel of Abduction.*

Philip Mantle and Paul Stonehill. *Russia's USO Secrets: Unidentified Submersible Objects in Russian and International Waters*

David Marler. *Triangular UFOs: An Estimate of the Situation.*

Lori McDonald, *Help for the Haunted: A Guide to House Blessings, Ghost Clearings, and Spiritual Self-Protection.*

Richard Sauder, Ph.D. *Hidden in Plain Sight: Beyond the X-Files.*

Ryan Sprague. *Somewhere in the Skies: A Human Approach to*

an Alien Phenomenon

Robert M. Wood, Ph.D. *Alien Viruses: Crashed UFOs, MJ-12, & Biowarfare.*

For these and other releases, visit
http://richarddolanpress.com

Made in the USA
Lexington, KY
06 August 2017